DIRECT THEORY

DIRECT THEORY

Experimental Motion Pictures as Major Genre

SECOND EDITION

Edward S. Small and Timothy W. Johnson

Southern Illinois University Press
Carbondale

16   15   14   13   4   3   2   1

Library of Congress Cataloging-in-Publication Data
Small, Edward S., date
Direct theory : experimental motion pictures as ma-
jor genre / Edward S. Small and Timothy W. Johnson.
— Second edition.
    pages cm
Includes bibliographical references and index.
ISBN-13: 978-0-8093-3213-7 (pbk. : alk. paper)
ISBN-10: 0-8093-3213-2 (pbk. : alk. paper)
ISBN-13: 978-0-8093-3214-4 (ebook)
ISBN-10: 0-8093-3214-0 (ebook)
1. Experimental films—History and criticism. I. John-
son, Timothy W., date. II. Title.
PN1995.9.E96S62 2013
791.43'611—dc23   2012046287

Printed on recycled paper. ♻
The paper used in this publication meets the minimum requirements of American National Standard
for Information Sciences—Permanence of Paper for
Printed Library Materials, ANSI Z39.48-1992. ∞

For Raymond Fielding

Art is thinking in images.

—*Victor Shklovsky*

Contents

Acknowledgments

A portion of chapter 2 was previously published in a different form in Edward S. Small, "Film and Video Art," in *Film and the Arts in Symbiosis*, edited by Gary Edgerton (New York: Greenwood Press, 1988, an imprint of Greenwood Publishing Group, Inc., Westport, Conn.); published by permission.

Edward S. Small wrote the first edition of this book but invited Timothy W. Johnson to be coauthor of the second edition, to work principally on the introduction and chapter 7.

We are grateful for the professional editorial assistance of copy editor Julie Bush and the front cover design by Mary Rohrer. The front cover illustration is from *Lines Horizontal Lines Vertical* (2012) by W. S. Cheng and is provided courtesy of W. S. Cheng.

DIRECT THEORY

Introduction

A number of interesting digital technological developments have occurred since the publication of the first edition (written in 1994 and republished in 1999 with a few corrections and edits), making it appropriate to update the book with Timothy W. Johnson. In fact, the subtitle of the first edition, *Experimental Film/ Video as Major Genre*, now must be expanded because many new experimental works are digital and may not use either film or video, hence the new subtitle: *Experimental Motion Pictures as Major Genre*. Considering that *Direct Theory*'s historiographical methodology followed Raymond Fielding's "technological determinism," this is an important task.

Fielding

In 1965, Fielding moved from UCLA to the film program at the University of Iowa, where Small met him in the fall of 1967 when he arrived at Iowa to begin his doctoral work. Over the next few years, Fielding taught Small film history, Japanese film, and animation history. These courses were to have a powerful influence upon him. Indeed, Small wrote his doctoral dissertation on Japanese animated film, which allowed him to begin understanding Fielding's "technological film history" as his methodology. To be sure, the very term "technological film history" likely comes from a 1985 publication by Robert C. Allen and Douglas Gomery that provided film scholars with an introduction to historiography. Their *Film History: Theory and Practice* offered a terse overview of many extant historiographical approaches in such chapters as "Aesthetic Film History" (which includes a section called "Masterpiece Tradition"), "Economic Film History" (which begins with a section called "The Marxist Critique"),

"Social Film History" (which includes a section called "The History of Film as a Cultural Document"), and "Technological Film History," which includes what Allen and Gomery call "Technological Determinism," highlighting the work of Fielding. Allen and Gomery's key quotation from Fielding comes from a 1980 essay of his published in *Sound and the Cinema*: "All my work as an historian, at least in recent years, has proceeded from the premise that the history of the motion picture—as an art form, as a medium of communication, and as an industry—has been determined principally by technological innovations and considerations."[1]

In the introduction to his *Technological History of Motion Pictures and Television*, Fielding sets out the premises for the methodological concept that Small later named *technostructure*:

> There is a temptation for film historians in particular to interpret the development of the motion picture teleologically, as if each generation of workers had sketched out the future of the art far in advance of the technology required for its realization. In fact, however, the artistic evolution of the film has always been intimately associated with technological change, just as it has, in less noticeable fashion, in the older arts. Just as the painter's art has changed with the introduction of different media and processes, just as the forms of symphonic music have developed with the appearance of new kinds of instruments, so has the elaboration and refinement of film style followed from the introduction of more sophisticated machinery. The contribution of a Porter, Ince, or Griffith followed as much from the availability of portable cameras and improved emulsions as it did from their individual vision and talent. Similarly, the cinema verité movement of today could not possibly have appeared and prospered twenty years ago, prior to the miniaturization of camera and sound equipment, and without dramatic improvements in film stocks.[2]

Today, Fielding is Dean Emeritus of Florida State University's College of Motion Picture Arts (from which he retired in 2003). His scholarship includes over half a dozen books, of which many are explicit examples of his technological methodology, such as *The Technique of Special Effects Cinematography* and *The American Newsreel: 1911–1967*.

Saussure

Just as Fielding is our key card for historiographical methodology, Ferdinand de Saussure is the key card for theoretical methodology. Saussure was the Swiss philologist/linguist whose posthumously published *Course in General Linguistics* provided the foundation for continental "cinesemiotics," especially in the work of Roland Barthes, Umberto Eco, and Christian Metz, who were quick to realize that Saussure's *patron general* of linguistics as well as his coinage of the term *semiology* opened the doors to a semiotic understanding of cinema. Saussure's teachings were, remarkably, derived from the notes of students who had taken his course in general linguistics, which he had taught at the University of Geneva between 1906 and 1911. To the best of our knowledge, Saussure's cited ideas were from his mind alone. Given the fact that these ideas remain revolutionary to this present day, it must be pointed out that his vision of what he came to call semiology not only was original but also remains counterintuitive for most contemporary American scholars. The following quotation reveals how prescient was his research, his thinking:

> *A science that studies the life of signs within society* is conceivable; it would be a part of social psychology and consequently of general psychology; I shall call it *semiology* (from Greek *semeion* "sign"). Semiology would show what constitutes signs, what laws govern them. Since the science does not yet exist, no one can say what it would be; but it has a right to existence, a place staked out in advance. Linguistics is only a part of the general science of semiology; the laws discovered by semiology will be applicable to linguistics, and the latter will circumscribe a well-defined area within the mass of anthropological facts.[3]

When Saussure's address is melded with Fielding's, the result is Small's concept of *technostructure*. That is, it incorporates Fielding's historiography, slightly altered, and adds to it Saussure's semiotic axiom that any change on the plane of the "signifier" (here the tangible, technical motion picture construction) is inextricably interwoven with changes on the plane of the "signified" (the thought, concept, or "content" occasioned by an individual's perception of a given semiotic unit). That is, there are no mere technological changes. Any technological change—to varying degrees, and for better or worse—brings with it structural consequence. The digital revolution likely constitutes the greatest technological change in the history of motion picture signifiers, and it will necessarily produce correlative changes in our "signifieds."

Allow us to iterate this particular Saussurian contention from the *Course in General Linguistics* that there can be no divorce of what he called "signifiers" (for example, these words on these pages that you, the reader, now process) and "signifieds" (that is, the concepts—perhaps "mentation" is a better word—that those signifiers occasion). This remains a revolutionary idea for semiotics in general, and for linguistics in particular. For Saussure there is no real synonymy because "in [semiotics] there are only differences. . . . There are no pre-existing ideas, and nothing is distinct before the appearance of language. . . . Language can also be compared with a sheet of paper: thought is the front and the sound the back; one cannot cut the front without cutting the back at the same time; one can neither divide sound [signifier] from thought [signified] nor thought from sound; the division could be accomplished only abstractly, and the result would be either pure psychology or pure phonology."[4]

And Saussure directly argues against latent Platonism when he writes, "If words stood for pre-existing concepts, they would all have exact equivalents in meaning from one language to the next; but this is not true. . . . Instead of pre-existing ideas then, we find that the concepts are purely differential and defined not by their positive content but negatively by their relations with the other terms of the system. Their most precise characteristic is in being what the others are not."[5]

Today there is a striking heuristic formula that one can find in various forms and various academic references dedicated to explicating Saussure's unique linguistic/semiotic insights:[6]

$$\text{Sign} = \frac{\text{Signified}}{\text{Signifier}}$$

Again, for Saussure, any change on the level of the signifier is inextricably bound to changes on the plane of the signified. This is remarkably consistent with *Direct Theory*'s historiography. For example,

Small recalls a personal discussion with Raymond Fielding about the exchange of cellulose acetate ("safety") film for the earlier, far more flammable and potentially explosive cellulose nitrate. "That was the real silver-screen," Fielding said. "The image truly scintillated." For Fielding, a technological change designed to increase safety resulted in an unplanned aesthetic change. The injunction against yelling "fire" in a crowded theater is still in common usage, although cellulose nitrate has not been available since the 1950s. We contend that the difference between these film stocks is comparable to the difference between water colors and oils, or perhaps between an original black-and-white photograph and a common black-and-white photocopy of it: the difference is quite consequential. Fielding's argument is, in other words, much the same as Saussure's. What is original in our contribution is but the melding of the two, as well as the applying of that particular blend to one of the three major categories of motion pictures, a good metaterm that Fielding also seems to favor, perhaps because it can cover celluloid film, that portable extension of broadcast television called video, and the current digital revolution. We call these three major categories *major genres.*

This, then, is a book of theory. It is also a book of history because of the conviction that only a diachronic regard for experimental motion pictures provides proper appreciation for the works that will be discussed in the following chapters. This conviction comes from almost four decades of teaching university undergraduate and graduate students—most of them film/video majors—about experimental production. With few exceptions, these students depended upon a historical survey for any real insights into the distinct forms and functions that characterize the development of experimental motion pictures from the 1920s to the present day. In a sense, these remarkable film/video/digital works create a dialogue one with the other, an intertextual investigation of highly theoretical issues that currently spans about nine decades. However, in both cases—as either theory or history—this book must be selective.

The historical selectivity that follows is the product of two simple factors. One is personal. Out of the countless experimental productions available to contemporary scholars, we have chosen to examine those we know best and believe best exemplify our thesis of direct theory. (Even here, we have had to reject, ignore, and overlook a great many significant artists and titles for the sake of proportion.) The other historiographical factor is also simple. With the exception of some reconfigurations (and is some cases, retitling) of genres, plus the more innovative melding of cinematographic and videographic and digital technologies, little that follows will attempt any real revision of extant historical regards. That is, we have employed what might well be called a canonical history of experimental production, a synthesis of established accounts by Sheldon Renan, David Curtis, Standish Lawder, P. Adams Sitney, Gene Youngblood, and Malcolm Le Grice. These writings (and others by Jonas Mekas, Stephen Dwoskin, William C. Wees, Robert Russett and Cecile Starr, Jonathan Price, and so on) constitute the academic foundations for this major genre. Doubtless, significant revision of that same history is in order and will appear in the years ahead, especially given the premise that we are but on the cusp of the "digital revolution."

This book is also designed to follow and fit within the parameters of established academic film theory, from its classic period through semiotics and contemporary poststructuralism into current cognitive science. Again, selectivity will mark our design. On the one hand, we will attend only to certain aspects of select figures throughout this tradition of written film theory; on the other hand, a number of currently popular schools of written theory simply do not seem to serve our direct theory thesis. Marxist, feminist, and psychoanalytic regards are key examples. In the main, their theoretical foundations are metamethodologic for the stuff and substance of the experimental productions to which they are often applied. Thus, we believe that they are of more value to the academic critic than most pure theory is. This distinction between motion picture criticism and theory is clarified in chapter 1.

Our historical interweave of experimental motion picture production and scholarly discourse is designed to present (and to validate) three interrelated original theses. First, this category of production cannot be subordinated under better-known categories such as the fictive narrative (that is, those theatrical features that clearly dominate cinema for both popular audiences and scholars) or the documentary (also known as nonfiction, actuality, and factual production). *Direct*

Theory contends that the experimental motion picture is a coordinate category and that its aesthetic is best understood when it is considered as a major genre coordinate to (but separate from) other major genres like fictive features and documentaries. This thesis constitutes a scholarly revision of most extant genre theory.

Direct Theory's second thesis is its explicit linking of the long history of experimental film with the more recent, briefer history of what is often termed *art video*. That is, from a technostructural regard, both categories of production are very similar in contradistinction to other modes of expression (such as novels or theater or painting). Eight technical/structural characteristics are employed to substantiate this (quite revisionist) thesis: acollaborative construction, economic independence, brevity, an affinity for ongoing technological developments, an affinity for the phenomenology of mental images, an avoidance of verbal language, an exploration of nonnarrative structures, and a pronounced (often quintessential) reflexivity—that is, much of the address of experimental production constitutes neither fictive entertainment nor documentary information but rather the very stuff and substance of the artwork itself: hence the name *Direct Theory*.

Finally, experimental motion pictures' remarkable reflexivity helps allow this often overlooked, greatly misunderstood major genre to function as a type of theory, a manifest, immediate, direct theory that bypasses the limiting intervention of separate semiotic systems, especially the spoken or written language upon which the accepted history of film theory depends. This final thesis may prove the most controversial in that our culture implicitly equates discourse with logos.

Beyond (or beside) these theoretical theses is a careful chronological overview that should serve as a thorough text for college courses devoted to the history of its subject. *Direct Theory* is designed as a historical/theoretical survey of that body of international motion pictures typically termed experimental or avant-garde. The book's seven chapters survey the entire development of this major genre, covering its beginnings in the European avant-garde, examining American underground production and international structuralist work (first in film and then in video), and then ending with experimental digital works that take the readers into this new millennium.

In this fashion, we are testing Fielding's historiography. The very vastness of this digital revolution has begun to manifest itself in experimental motion pictures. As scholars and students witnessed the shift first from film proper to video, it is our goal to explore digital experimental works in chapter 7. In fact, in the *Journal of Film and Video* (Spring/Summer 2005), Small published an article, "Techno-structural Expectations," which came out of his constant search for just such a manifestation. Then five years later, his teaching assistant, Richard Housh, discovered the first evidence for those expectations.

The reader should be aware of the various distribution centers, rental libraries, and archives that provide easy access to most of the works discussed in the following pages: Canyon Cinema, 145 Ninth Street, Suite 260, San Francisco, Calif., 94103, http://canyoncinema.com/; The Film-Makers' Cooperative, 475 Park Avenue South, 6th Floor, New York, N.Y., 10016, http://www.film-makerscoop.com/; Circulating Film and Video Library, The Museum of Modern Art, 11 West 53rd Street, New York, N.Y., 10019, http://www.moma.org/learn/resources/circulatingfilm; and Electronic Arts Intermix, 535 West 22nd Street, 5th Floor, New York, N.Y., 10011, http://www.eai.org/index.htm.

In addition, the Internet is a rich and accessible source. Nearly all of the films (or at least excerpts from them) discussed in this book can be found there.

1. Experimental Motion Pictures as Direct Theory

Contemporary film/video curricula and pedagogy recognize a dichotomy between coursework in production and coursework in three scholarly areas: criticism, history, and theory. To be sure, these same distinctions are often served by overlapped boundaries. Production skills can inform critical skills, for example, which can reciprocally inform creativity. Likewise, few historical analyses are completely removed from critical and/or theoretical concerns. (We will see this quite clearly when we attend to the historical surveys of Sheldon Renan, David Curtis, Standish Lawder, Malcolm Le Grice, and others.) Such overlap is particularly prominent between the areas of criticism and theory, especially today when most academic criticism rests upon explicit or implicit theoretical methodologies.

Nonetheless, pure theory remains distinct from most criticism. Criticism's concern is typically the explication and evaluation of select film/video texts. Theory, in contrast, typically employs select aspects of various film/video texts in order to explicate general qualities, which in turn helps us delineate those elements and functions that are intrinsic and extrinsic to the medium under analysis. As Dudley Andrew's *The Major Film Theories* suggests, "The goal, then, of film theory is to formulate a schematic notion of the capacity of film."[1]

Especially in its classic period, film theory is a very well delineated body of literature. Following the pioneer efforts of Hugo Munsterberg's *The Photoplay: A Psychological Study* and Vachel Lindsay's *The Art of the Moving Picture* (both first published in 1916), film theory evolved into what is today termed the Eisenstein-Bazin debate. This debate is predicated upon two contesting regards, two polar values for the same phenomena: the cinematographic capacities for both the transformation and the reproduction of reality.

The debate began in the late 1920s with the writings (and pro-duction) of a number of Russian formalists, including Lev Kuleshov and Sergei Eisenstein. Eisenstein's well-translated and well-published writings (especially *Film Form* and *The Film Sense*) came to champion the transformational properties of editing—an element intrinsic to film for which Eisenstein provided the neologism *montage*. A great number of theorists can be grouped within this transformational school, including Kuleshov, Vsevolod Pudovkin, Béla Balázs, and the German-born Rudolf Arnheim, whose continually reprinted 1933 *Film as Art* clearly extends the transformational properties of mon-tage into all elements of cinema: composition, sound, color, camera speeds, lighting, and so forth.

The foil to the remarkably coherent transformational premises that marked film theory in the 1920s and 1930s appeared after the Second World War with the work of André Bazin. In contradistinction to prior theory, Bazin came to devalue film's transformational resources by contending that cinema's ability to reproduce reality was in fact its major asset, not its aesthetic liability. Bazin's address was very philosophical, arguing in such essays as "The Ontology of the Photo-graphic Image" that photographs (and, by extension, cinematographic images) "share a common being, after the fashion of a finger print," with those subjects they can so faithfully record.[2] Bazin's reproduc-tive values later came to be shared by a number of theorists such as Siegfried Kracauer, whose 1960 publication of *Theory of Film* preceded the translation in 1967 of Bazin's *What Is Cinema?* into English.

As late as the beginning of the 1970s, American film theory was largely constituted by partisan scholarship upon these two seemingly contradictory schools. Further, while the academic discipline of film theory clearly excluded the criticism of, say, Pauline Kael or even Andrew Sarris, it still retained a highly normative, prescriptive/pro-scriptive posture. Then, with the 1974 publication of Christian Metz's *Film Language: A Semiotics of the Cinema*, the discipline received a distinctly descriptive regard that proved broad enough to encompass, and thereby resolve, this classic Eisenstein-Bazin debate.

Drawing upon the posthumous publication of Ferdinand de Saus-sure's *Course in General Linguistics* (1915, based upon lectures at the Uni-versity of Geneva between 1906 and 1911), Metz and other semioticians' linking of linguistics with film theory's schematic goal was itself hardly new. Lindsay had likened film's images to hieroglyphics, Eisenstein had constructed elaborate comparisons between Japanese and Chinese pictographs and montage, and even Bazin had spoken of film as a language. What did make Metz's work distinct was his more scientific (more descriptive as opposed to prescriptive) employ of Saussure's prescient vision of a science of all sign systems, a science that depended upon the privileged position of linguistics. Saussure predicted that "semiology would show what constitutes signs, what laws govern them."[3]

A half-century after Saussure's death, Metz and other continental cinesemioticians like Umberto Eco introduced into American film theory a new perspective that did not so much fault as supersede, not so much replace as encompass the earlier, seemingly contradictory but now complementary transformational and reproductive schools. And the key to this new perspective was Saussure's distinct concept of the sign as a relational (as opposed to a substantive, tangible) entity. For theorists like Metz, Saussure's concept of sign was clearly translinguistic (including, by implication, such diverse systems as garments, gestures, paintings, photos) and thus provided promise for unique insights into both cinematography and videography. Indeed, by drawing upon Saussure's definition of syntagm, Metz came to catalog and categorize eight main types of montage configurations, which he called the *grande syntagmatique*.[4] This accomplishment at once transcended the prescriptive/proscriptive values placed upon montage by Eisenstein and Bazin and—in keeping with Saussure's regard for signs as constitutive as opposed to nominative entities—redefined (and helped resolve) Bazin's ontological arguments.

In our present period, American film theory has come to witness the special extension of Saussure's insights into poststructuralism. Poststructuralism lacks cinesemiotics' implicit faith in an eventual "schematic notion" of film/video "laws." Also, poststructuralist approaches (such as contemporary deconstruction) have reblurred the academic distinctions between criticism and theory, while their interdisciplinary premises have reformed film theory into a far broader vantage that is often termed simple *theory*. Saussure's influence still marks many poststructuralist writings, though he has often become more foil than mentor.

11

This history and development of written film theory is thus academically well established. Strictly speaking, film theory is precisely this established body of extant, academically accepted texts. How, then, can a given body of film (and, later, video) production be said to fit and follow this same tradition? As Andrew argues in *The Major Film Theories*, "No one would equate a film theory, which after all is merely an order of words, with the experience of a film."[5] While certain theorists such as Eisenstein constructed highly innovative films that were at once an experimental application of their written theory as well as the very basis for much of those same theoretical writings, the tradition of film theory has always kept these two modes quite separate. Theory, by (implicit) definition—either axiomatic or tautologic—is dependent upon verbal discourse (perhaps spoken, usually written), even if augmented by charts or diagrams or photographic illustrations.

This question of a given body of production being able to function as theory may in fact be two interrelated questions. The first attends to the perhaps arbitrary tradition of film theory's reliance upon words as its main semiotic device. Just as a theory in the discipline of physics would depend upon traditional numbers and formulae as its major semiotic resource, just as (the distinct form and function of) music theory depends upon an elaborate semiotic system of notes and other devices that constitute musical scores and related articulation, film theory has traditionally—though not exclusively—depended upon philosophical exposition. Eisenstein's writings alone reveal exceptions. His prose often borders upon fragmented free verse, while his diagrams and his photographic illustrations depend upon distinct semiotic systems. Thus, this primary question of tradition is not without some promising gaps for an argument supporting direct theory.

But a second, more fundamental question remains: how can the semiotic system of images (cinematographic, videographic, or digital, likely accompanied by sounds but for the sake of this question no pertinent written or spoken words) function as that mode of philosophic discourse we regard as theoretical? This is a very complex issue to which this entire book is devoted. Indeed, it constitutes this book's main thesis, and we suspect it will prove a controversial one. Only the many specific examples of this mode of theory that we have termed *direct* and that occupy the chapters that follow can in any real way begin to address and answer this core question. At this juncture, we only seek to set before our readers some premises that, while provisional, will find progressive embodiment throughout our historical survey. In the following chapters, we examine a type of film and video production that we contend does not function mainly as (fictive) popular entertainment or as (documentary) information. Its major function is rather to theorize upon its own substance by reflecting back on its own intrinsic semiotic system(s).

First, allow us to point out again that for at least some written theorists, the notion that images per se can operate as a mode of discourse was quite acceptable. Eisenstein (though political pressures later brought about his recanting) began his writings with this very vision, his quest for a cinematographic analog to philosophical discourse:

> Now why should the cinema follow the forms of theatre and painting rather than the methodology of language, which allows wholly new concepts of ideas to arise from the combination of two concrete denotations of two concrete objects? Language is much closer to film than painting is. For example, in painting the form arises from *abstract* elements of line and color, while in cinema the material *concreteness* of the image within the frame presents—as an element—the greatest difficulty in manipulation. So why not rather lean toward the system of language, which is forced to use the same mechanics in inventing words and word-complexes?[6]

Decades later, Rudolf Arnheim's book *Visual Thinking*—the very title of which could beg rebuttal as oxymoronic—came to contend that even pre-photographic percepts already carried out the task of high-level mentation. "My contention is that the cognitive operations called thinking are not the privilege of mental processes above and beyond perception but the essential ingredients of perception itself. I am referring to such operations as active exploration, selection, grasping of essentials, simplification, abstraction, analysis and synthesis, completion, correction, comparison, problem solving, as well as combing, separating, putting in context."[7]

The Greek etymology for *theory* is, after all, hardly intrinsic to verbal discourse: *theoria*, "a looking at." Can there not be modes of motion pictures that are devoted to "looking at" the kinds of questions and concerns that have historically marked written film theory? One such concern is the issue of medium specificity. While cinema has doubtless exhibited pronounced relationships to theater, the novel, painting, music, or journalistic investigation (documentation and reportage), are such relationships intrinsic or extrinsic to the cinematographic medium? Not only is this a perennial question for written theory, but it would seem to be a question that would profit greatly from a mode of inquiry uncontaminated by the semiotic system of verbal discourse—a system that precisely marks much theater, all novels, and most journalism. Could Arnheim be correct when, in his extension of concepts to pictures, he argues, "In sum, every pictorial analogue performs the task of reasoning"?[8] Could images themselves provide high-level cognitive functions, functions that could bypass the potentially muddy mediation of linguistic signs?

As early as 1967, Michael Gazzaniga published "The Split Brain in Man," which proved to be a watershed empirical insight into what is today known as *cortical asymmetry*. This *Scientific American* article concluded with a provocative insight: "All the evidence indicates that separations of the [brain] hemispheres creates two independent spheres of consciousness within a single cranium, that is to say, within a single organism. This conclusion is disturbing to some people who view consciousness as an indivisible property of the human brain."[9] Gazzaniga's foundation for over four succeeding decades of empirical research supported Arnheim's concept of visual thinking, although by and large restricting it to the right brain hemisphere. Whereas the left hemisphere is mainly devoted to semiotic systems like words and numbers, the right hemisphere's province encompasses modes like music and maps—plus cinematographic, videographic, and digital images.

This is not to say that such specific cortical processes must rely upon any mediation from left-brain functions. We suspect that many scholars who are today quite familiar with the basic insights from cortical asymmetry research still harbor—perhaps naively, perhaps from a far more covert, doctrinaire axiom—the notion that any real mentation must ultimately derive from left-brain resources. As we shall see, Jacques Derrida's deconstruction regards such a crucial conviction as "logocentric" and (by design or by default) as a kind of philosophic hegemony.

Postmodernist deconstruction derives from the much earlier semiotics of Saussure, whose *Course in General Linguistics* made a prescient "remark in passing":

> [W]hen semiology becomes organized as a science, the question will arise whether or not it properly includes modes of expression based on completely natural signs, such as pantomime. Supposing that the new science welcomes them, its main concern will still be the whole group of systems grounded on the arbitrariness of the sign. In fact, every means of expression used in society is based, in principle, on collective behavior or—what amounts to the same thing—on convention. . . . Signs that are wholly arbitrary realize better than the others the ideal of the semiological process; that is why language, the most complex and universal of all systems of expression, is also the most characteristic; in this sense linguistics can become the master-pattern for all branches of semiology although language is only one particular semiological system.[10]

Saussure's logocentric privilege for written/spoken language here is a curious one. To be sure, his real concern was the arbitrary bonding between a linguistic sign's signifier and signified. Conversely, the far more "motivated" bonding of "natural signs" (Saussure's "visual signifiers"), which he termed *symbols*, received remarkably meager address in his *Course*. A symbol, he went on to briefly address, had "one characteristic" of being "never wholly arbitrary; it is not empty for there is the rudiment of a natural bond between the signifier and the signified."[11]

First, we would rush to point out that the respective terms *form* and *content* would be devious synonyms for Saussure's signifier/ signified because these still fashionable (contemporary) terms are interconnected with distinctly contradictory models of signification (for example, where form is conceived of as quite separable from content). Second, even Saussure's logocentrism did not incorporate the sense that a symbol in any way depended upon a sign's media-tion. While linguistics would indeed prove a "master pattern" for, say, later cinesemiotics, the signifiers of the motion-picture image are directly interconnected with a given viewer's signifieds. Indeed, since for Saussure even words within the same language could by definition never be true synonyms (any change on the plane of signifier being inextricably interconnected to some change on the plane of signified), lack of synonymy is even more pronounced between languages (the words *dog* and *hund* and *chien* and *inu* are distinctly interwoven with English, German, French, and Japanese cultures).

When we get to the level of different semiotic systems, this es-sential Saussurian rejection of classic and contemporary models of communication becomes only greater. A word like *dog* and a photo of a dog are vastly different. (From the perspective of contemporary cortical asymmetry, they are quite literally processed by different brains.) Further, and most important, the photograph can be pro-cessed without any recourse to logocentrically proposed verbal me-diation. (Of course, both modes can work in tandem, alternately or augmentively—but that is a separate issue.) Here we have the key to Saussure's revolutionary rejection of still lingering Platonic models for mentation and signification: "Without language, thought is a vague, uncharted nebula. There are no pre-existing ideas, and nothing is distinct before the appearance of language."[12] In sum, each sign or symbol articulates one's phenomenology in a distinct manner, and—from the perspective of Saussure's structuralism—what Arnheim came to call visual thinking is by definition independent of left-brain mediation. Saussure's symbolic articulation can readily be regarded as right-brain specific.

Much can be made of the linguistic concept of articulation when addressing the fundamental questions of image discourse. It is only by metaphoric extension that we employ *articulation* as a rough syn-onym for *speech*. Basically, articulation attends to those joints that constitute any connected parts—such as the phonemes of speech or the human arm's elbow (as when a physician checks such articulation after an injury) or the articles in a journal. And cinesemiotics was to find some such articulation in the system of motion pictures precisely where Eisenstein had found it decades before—within the montage interstices that are the foundation of Metz's *grande syntagmatique.* Other cinesemioticians such as Umberto Eco have sought schematic descriptions of intrashot articulation. The concept of discourse is crucial here; for, as Jung realized, discrimination is the essence of consciousness. Semiotic articulation perhaps describes, perhaps constitutes discrimination, but in either case, discourse occurs in the two Saussurian provinces: sign and symbol.

Roland Barthes, whose "semiological adventure" autobiographically recounts the way he (and Metz and Eco) entered Saussure's meager passage from sign to symbol, appropriately employs "discourse" in a manner revisionist to its spoken/written confine: "Language, or to be more precise, *discourse* has been the constant object of my work, since my first book."[13] "A garment, an automobile, a dish of cooked food, a *film*, a piece of music, an advertising image, a piece of furniture, a newspaper, headline. . . . What might they have in common? This at least: all are signs."[14] While Barthes here ignores the discriminatory power of the precise Saussurian term *symbol,* his well-known applications of Saussure to such diverse semiotic systems as costume, cuisine, and cinema clearly help us extend our very concept of discourse— interwoven, as it is, with the faculty of human reason—beyond the standard articulations provided by both speech and writing.

Barthes also ignores the major genre of experimental film and video production and therefore does not even consider that such production could itself constitute a kind of theory. By and large, we stand alone in this position, although (as we shall see) other writers on this major genre have expressed views that have encouraged us and to which we are indebted. Malcolm Le Grice, for example, ends his (very theoretical) *Abstract Film and Beyond* with the following:

[T]he abstract and formal cinema seeks clarification within the films themselves of the relationship between the subjectivity of the film-maker, the constraints of his "language" and the subjectivity of the film-viewer. The search for this clarity of means, coupled with the attempt to give to the spectator an affirmation of his own reality[,] has led to the emergence of deliberately reflexive forms. Thirdly, therefore, it seeks to counteract the emotional manipulation and reactionary catharsis of popular cinematic form by the development of conscious, conceptual and reflexive modes of perception thus representing the most advanced and radical state of cinematic language and convention.[15]

Perhaps most encouraging was the late Christian Metz, whose post–*grande syntagmatique* interest in experimental film/video as well as his critiques of some of Small's research resulted in an invaluable insight that helped us resolve the problematic relationships between written and direct theory: "I completely agree with you that experimental cinema . . . and experimental video . . . are forms of theory, which cannot replace the written theory, but cannot be replaced by it either."[16]

What, then, is the relationship between the written theory and direct theory surveyed in the chapters that follow? We do not believe it is a strictly causal, seriatim relationship. On the one hand, the written theory of Eisenstein, Bazin, Arnheim, Kracauer, Metz, and others evidences an intertextuality with the historical (*cum* critical/theoretical) writings by experimental artists themselves (for example, Stan Brakhage) and with those academic foundations for this major genre: books by Renan, Curtis, Youngblood, Sitney, and others. On the other hand, the relationship between all this written theory and the direct theory of our select film/video productions seems, in the main, acausal. While at times one mode may comment upon, react to, or even anticipate the other, what we will see is an ever-shifting intercausation of parts and principles. Vast interrelationships seem to exist between written theory and direct theory, but simple causality can in no way even begin to account for them. They are rather systemic, synergetic, and intertransformative; they suggest Jung's concept of synchronicity (his "a-causal connecting principle") far more than any classic concept of either cause or concomitance.[17] Metz seems quite correct: both written theory and direct theory are mutually irreplaceable. We would only add that their intercommunity is so complex that it will probably remain beyond any semiotic mapping.

A complementary regard that falls just short of our concept of direct theory is Scott MacDonald's *A Critical Cinema*. MacDonald does see critical cinema as having one approach "most nearly *theoretical*" not in its relationship to written theory but rather in relation to "conventional cinema": "[I]nstead of foregrounding recognizable characters and narratives, the [experimental] theoretical films foreground the mechanical, chemical, perceptual, and conceptual structures that underlie the theatrical film experience in general."[18]

For all of these collected insights, we suspect most film and video theoreticians today would rather contend that theory and verbal/ written language are axiomatically and quite exclusively cojoined. However, we hope to have shown that not all contemporary theoreticians would so agree. Deconstructionists like Derrida would rather suggest that such a "commonsense" position derives from a subtle logocentrism that makes it more tautologic than axiomatic. To be clear, when we write that certain kinds of film and video works constitute a mode of theory, theory direct, without the mediation of a separate semiotic system, we do not mean that these works reflect or exemplify theories, nor do we mean that they employ various theoretical issues as themes. Instead, we are seeking the reader's (at least provisional) abandonment of any logocentric model that would make right-hemispheric visual thinking dependent upon any mediation by left-hemispheric words. Saussure's symbols, like his signs, are inextricable bondings of signifier and signified. Experimental film and video productions can thus function as a mode of theory quite directly.

2. Experimental Motion Pictures as Major Genre

E xperimental productions at once suffer and enjoy a marginal
position throughout the history of motion picture scholarship.
While these productions constitute a remarkably coherent genre,
that genre remains an unusually overlooked one. However, this same
marginality provides a peculiar site, an especially heuristic vantage
from which to question a number of critical concepts that have
marked the history of motion picture scholarship. Just as Western
music's arbitrary traditions become clearer from the oppositional
contrast of Indian music, or just as Western philosophy is more
readily deconstructed from the distinct perspectives of Indo-Asian
philosophy, so too can established critical concepts of motion pictures
be examined and interrogated from experimental cinema's marginality. Indeed, this vantage is similar to Scott MacDonald's concept
of "a critical cinema":

> The most interesting and useful film-critical insights of recent
> years, it could be argued, have been coming not from the con-
> tinuing elaborations of auteurism and genre studies or from
> the systematic application of recent French theory to popular
> film, but from that remarkable body of North American films
> known variously as "underground film," "the New American
> Cinema," "experimental cinema," and "avant-garde cinema."
> Many of if not most of the filmmakers loosely designated by
> such terms explicitly and implicitly view the dominant, com-
> mercial cinema (and its sibling, television) not as a compet-
> ing mode but as a set of culturally conditioned and accepted
> approaches to cinema—a cultural text—*to be analyzed from
> within the medium of film itself.* One of the goals of these critical
> filmmakers has been to place our awareness and acceptance of

the commercial forms and their highly conventionalized modes of representation into crisis.[1]

MacDonald's paragraph mentions two critical mainstays, both of which will receive revisionist regard in this chapter. One of these mainstays is commonly known as *auteur theory*. With its roots in post–World War II France—especially select essays published during the 1950s in the cinema journal *Cahiers du cinema*—what was initially called *politique des auteurs* was transformed and popularized by the American film critic Andrew Sarris during the 1960s. The premises of auteur criticism are, first, that film is a highly collaborative art form (the product of writers, actors, cinematographers, editors, studios, directors, and so on) that contradicts the kind of artistic credit that society provides comparatively autonomous novelists or painters; and second, that in certain films, certain directors' exceptional personalities can realize a thematic and stylistic impression that allows these directors to receive clear artistic credit for the film. Today, these still debatable premises inform a great deal of popular and even academic film categorization. To speak of going to see a Woody Allen film or a new Steven Spielberg film has become a societal commonplace.

The second critical mainstay that will receive revisionist regard throughout this book is commonly known as *genre theory*. Basically, it is derived from a proto-empirical faith in the powers of categorization to aid our understanding of phenomena. Faced with countless film titles, film criticism was quick to construct such now-common categories as westerns, musicals, and horror films. In its more sophisticated academic form, such categorization is proposedly interrelated with audience expectations. In its simplest form, such categorization rather depends upon rude distinctions of subject matter (as one might find in a children's library section titled "Sea Stories").

From the perspective of the pages that follow, the greatest weakness of most popular and academic generic categorization (the very phrase "generic categorization" being somewhat redundant, since the French word *genre* means "kind" or "type") is oversubordination. Because most of the genre theory that marks scholarly publication and academic curricula is devoted to subcategories of the fictive feature—those theatrical narratives that dominate movie houses and home viewing—such differential emphasis upon westerns, musicals, or the subject matter of war often results in troublesome tunnel vision that not only fails to recognize such equally robust major genres as experimental motion pictures but also, relatedly, fails to understand them: for recognition and understanding both are attendant upon structural considerations.

Oversubordination implicitly or explicitly relegates the distinct aesthetic address of experimental or documentary works to subcategories of the fictive narrative. This at once confounds the heuristic powers of proper classification (which depend upon taxonomic concerns with hierarchical patterns of coordination and subordination) and confounds our understanding of the alternate category that constitutes the subject of this book.

If we limit or revise the use of the term and concept *genre* to address major structural groupings, then the resulting profile is far broader and far clearer about coordination and subordination than is extant motion picture genre theory. Indeed, we would thus begin a proper taxonomy of motion picture productions. *Taxonomy* is a general science of classification (theory and practice). It deals with human concept formation with regard to a particular discipline. Its core concerns are both patterns of coordination (of the same order, rank, importance) and subordination (of lower order, rank, importance). Apart from the very important epistemological questions related to any classification theory—innate and/or arbitrary constructions of human categorical activity—are immediate pragmatic concerns. Does the resulting organization possess adequate heuristic power? Will the particular coordination and subordination allow ongoing insights into extant and future structures?

The very familiarity of the fictive feature makes it an excellent ground against which such alternate major genres as experimental production can be figured. It is cinema's "royal road," what people usually think of when they discuss motion pictures. One well-known coordinate category is the nonfiction motion picture (also called documentary and factual). Structurally, such works are distinct from fictive narratives because of a number of characteristics (typically briefer, often marked by voice-over narration, recording subjects that are real people in real places, and so son). Subordination is very well developed with propaganda works, newsreels, cinema verité, ethnographic productions, and the like. (Indeed, depending upon one's level of sophistication, subordination can continue through ever-increasing subsets: the newsreel, for example, further subordinates categories like the news series Kino Pravda, Warner-Pathé, and March of Time; March of Time evidences even further structural distinctions since some reels, for example, were multi-topic pieces while most later works were devoted to a single subject.) This brief overview hardly speaks to the scope and complexity of factual motion pictures, though it should help elevate them to a position coordinate with the fictive narrative. Unless such coordination is realized, unless both fictive features and documentaries are revisioned as major genres, the documentary motion picture can become spuriously subject to the same aesthetic expectations as the fictive feature, making it dull and arcane to both scholars and popular audiences.[2]

One purpose of this present book, then, is to comparably elevate experimental production. There are many reasons for this goal. For one, experimental work is, again, remarkably overlooked. In contrast to its coordinate major genres of actuality and fictive narrative, it suffers scholastic neglect at best and genuine hostility at worst, partly due to a largely naive (but at times perhaps doctrinaire) mis-subordination to the fictive feature. For another, while there may be countless reasons for experimental motion pictures' academic Coventry, one particular insight has come to clarify our understanding and constitutes the major thesis of this book. As discussed in chapter 1, these distinct productions—which typically stand outside industrial economics, are often quintessential auteur products, and seek structures beyond the commonplace narrative of fictive features or the almost omnipresent narration of documentaries—constitute a kind of theory. That is, unlike written motion picture theory, which depends upon the separate semiotic system of verbal language, experimental motion pictures' theoretical address transcends such clumsy mediation. And just as written theory hardly enjoys majority embrace or understanding, so too should one expect experimental works' at times hostile reception and audience perplexity. To a great extent, the real audiences for such works have been either fellow artists or a small body of specialized scholars.

This same thesis is a complex one that will develop as we survey the historic evolution of this major genre. For the present chapter, it is essential only that we establish this body of production as a major genre, coordinate to documentaries and fictive narratives and hosting its own elaborate subordination. With this task in mind, we offer figure 2.1. Consider its horizontal axis as the plane of generic coordination, while its vertical axis exemplifies some of the ultimately vast complexity that constitutes generic subordination. For our present purposes, we will deal only with three coordinate major genres; others could be added (television advertising commercials, film "trailers," and music videos come directly to mind).[3] The first subclass below the major genre line constitutes genres proper, consonant with that term's extant use; any further articulations are (provisionally) termed *subcategories*.

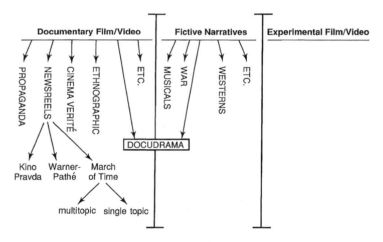

Figure 2.1. Major genres.

All such generic articulations are best regarded as a contemporary scholastic endeavor rather than matters of creative concerns by the artists themselves. Early cinema exhibits a comparative homogeneity that, in a sense, made all productions equally "experimental." (For example, demarcation of the documentary did not really begin until John Grierson coined the term for a 1926 review of Robert Flaherty's *Moana*.) Further, all distinction—all such articulation—may well be arbitrary. Consider optical distinctions between colors on the electromagnetic spectrum or more casual distinctions between brooks and streams and rills and rivers—all demand demarcation of a continuum. Even the distinction between male and female is confounded by androgyny. And just as a specialist in sexual anatomy may well find focus upon the blurred boundary of the hermaphrodite most instructive and most insightful into the nature and limitations of the very valuable and very valid categories of gender, so too does the film and video theorist find heuristic value in generic overlapping. Figure 2.1's "docudrama" is a transgeneric synthesis of both the fictive and documentary categories. Likewise, we shall later examine certain subclasses of experimental production that at once contest and question the major generic boundaries this chapter seeks to establish. These curiosities can be seen both as exceptions that make the rule and as paradoxes that promise privileged insights into the entire issue of human categorical activity. With such combined limitation and resource in mind, we offer eight provisional characteristics for the form experimental film/video, characteristics that underlie the basic articulation presented in figure 2.1.

The first of these is related to that critical mainstay with which we began this chapter, auteur theory. Currently, motion pictures are most often considered essentially collaborative arts. This regard has raised the complex issue of auteur credit, credit comparable to that which we provide poets, novelists, painters, and composers of music. However, experimental production has always been marked by a significant number of independent artists, such as filmmaker Stan Brakhage or video artist Bill Viola, who remain fully responsible for each and every aspect of their production—from conception to scripting, through shooting and editing, and often into distribution. By "fully responsible," we do not mean directorial *control* of these various components. Nor do we mean ensemble work under auteur direction. Our concern is genuine acollaborative control in which the artist performs each component task.

Whereas a typical fictive feature—regardless of auteur directorship—employs writers, cinematographers, editors, special effects personnel, sound and lighting technicians, and so on (and the list is an extensive one), the typical experimental artist is comparatively quite autonomous. The first real academic text devoted to this major genre, Sheldon Renan's 1967 *Introduction to the American Underground Film*, was quick to recognize the same characteristic. Renan wrote that such a work was "a film conceived and made essentially by one person and [as a result] is a *personal statement* by that person."[4] In our own research and writing, we have come to call this generic characteristic either *acollaborative construction* or *quintessential auteur control*. Under either label, it does challenge major premises of classic auteur theory.[5]

The second characteristic is indebted to a later historical survey of experimental production. David Curtis's *Experimental Cinema* details his concept of economic independence: works made outside the mutual support and constraints of industrial economics.[6] To Curtis's insight we would add only the qualification of grant support. Throughout the almost nine-decade history of this major genre, a great many of the motion pictures we will survey (and countless established classics we will omit) were dependent directly or indirectly upon grant support. (Oskar Fischinger's all but impoverished career provides a good, early example of this.) Doubtless, such competitive financial aid is not fully removed from political issues, aesthetic fashions, festival prizes, or museum distribution. Still, the comparative financial autonomy of the experimental artist has likely realized far more assets than liabilities. To be sure, some fictive and documentary works are comparably independent, but the situation of experimental/avant-garde production is so thoroughly disassociated from industry financing and distribution as well as from industry's structural and stylistic demands that this distinction rests upon matters far more consequential than those of degree.

Not unrelated to this same economic independence is the third characteristic, brevity. Here we have come to employ (as an arbitrary parameter) Renan's early insight that such works "are usually under thirty minutes in length."[7] Exceptions abound. Michael Snow's *La Region Central* (1971) greatly exceeds most fictive feature lengths. Further, the generic specificity of brevity is weak. Historically, the educational documentary rarely exceeded thirty minutes, and what may be the experimental/avant-garde film's briefest production—Bruce Conner's *Ten Second Film* (1965)—was the length of most common television advertising commercials of the era.

Indeed, no one of these eight generic characteristics can be considered necessary or sufficient for categorization. They are best regarded as systemic. Only if a "cluster" of such characteristics is apparent does a given work become a proper candidate for generic inclusion. Moreover, it would be a rare work that included all eight characteristics. Still, brevity does mark most of the productions we will survey, as does the fourth characteristic: an affinity for ongoing technological developments. This characteristic is also indebted to Renan, who claimed that the particular body of films he addressed—from early European avant-garde work through his own focus upon 1950s and 1960s American underground production—was a "hotbed of technical innovation."[8]

So drawn to such technical resource is experimental production that we can catalog not only an affinity for animation (see endnote 3), step printers, and what is typically called *special effects* (for example, split screens, distortion lenses, and so on) but also an eventual embrace of video technology and digital computers: the very reason why we have come to call this major genre "experimental motion pictures." Interrelated with this same elaborate panoply of technological resources is characteristic five: a penchant for the phenomenology of mental imagery. As we have seen, this particular phenomenology of artistic experience—being intrinsically insubstantial—came to be proscribed by one school of classic (written) film theory, namely, the post–World War II writings of Siegfried Kracauer and André Bazin. Perhaps both in contradistinction to and in doctrinaire defiance of this realist proscription, experimental production has almost always provided a place for an artist's exploration of dreams, reveries, hallucinations, hypnogogic imagery, and the like. And this major genre's affinity for technological resources provided much of the means for these artistic attempts to imitate, to try to somehow reconstruct this same fleeting phenomenology. While we cannot say that all experimental production has chosen to exchange the reproductive school's emphasis upon external vision for what Stan Brakhage has called "closed-eye vision," its penchant for experiences independent of external stimuli, for surrogates of mental imagery, is so much greater than fictive narrative's or documentary's that the difference is another matter of kind rather than of degree.

Characteristic six, an avoidance of verbal language, is also interconnected with experimental film/video's often pyrotechnic explorations of closed-eye visions. It is also likely interconnected with the characteristics of economic independence; for, at least in the realm of film, sound can prove prohibitively expensive. However, with later video constructions, sound carries little if any expense or additional technical expertise, and today's experimental motion pictures genre remains the only major genre that at times still chooses the simplicity of silence.[9] Mental imagery can be interwoven with aural phenomena, but such connection appears extrinsic. While the fictive feature has always depended upon intertitles and, later, spoken dialogue, and while the nonfiction film has either embraced the propagandist power of voice-over narration or cinema verité's predications upon portable direct sound, experimental production rather tends to eschew words—written, spoken as dialogue, or narrated. Even before the advent of workable sound in the 1930s, early avant-garde production evidenced less use of intertitles than did either actuality or fictive works from the same period. And once sound became available, clearly the greater proportion of experimental/avant-garde films (and, later, videos) employed only soundtracks of either music or effects. Well before current psychological theories of cortical asymmetry, experimental artists seemed to grasp the psychophysiological divorce between left and right hemispheric functions. Experimental motion pictures thus attend more to the right-brain hemisphere's specialization for imagery (in isolation from any competition with the left brain's specialization for verbal language). More, when exceptions to this characteristic are found, the attention to written/spoken language is so pronounced that it—quite in the power of paradox—often follows a distinctly reflexive function, directly deconstructing the very verbal language to which the work attends. Finally, this characteristic avoidance of verbal language appears interrelated with generic characteristic number seven: an exploration of nonnarrative structures.

While exceptions are legion, especially if one considers even a slender hint of story as evidence for narrativity, by and large experimental film/video is intentionally and theoretically opposed to that commonplace (and remarkably formulistic) narrative construction that remains the very substance of the fictive feature, from *The Birth of a Nation* to annual Academy Award winners. As Renan realized over forty years ago, "narratives are rare in the underground."[10]

With its classical continuity, the theatrical feature is marked by precise cinematographic and editing patterns (for example, matched action, no jump cuts, clear axis lines), which are interrelated with broader narrative elements shared by the classic novel (for example, characterization, point of view, and what Small has come to call a *fictive differential*, Christian Metz's distinction between a film's running time and the story's "diegetic" time).[11] The coordinate major genre of nonfiction/documentary production shares such constructions only in part and relies more upon voice-over narration for its particular narrativity. It is only the experimental major genre that eschews these narrative constructions for doctrinaire and quite theoretical purposes. More precisely, when experimental motion pictures do deal with narrative (and we will examine a number of such works that do so, in varying degrees), they typically present fragmented narratives that tend to confound the conventions of classical continuity; thus, these classic conventions stand either parodied or deconstructed by this major genre's function as direct theory. In this wise, experimental production's concern with narrative is largely reflexive, which brings us to our final and most complex characteristic.

Reflexivity is part and parcel of so many kinds of contemporary art that it should be easy to define. However, this formalist aesthetic strategy that returns audience attention to the actual construction of the artwork, which makes the artwork itself its own subject, is such a vast and ever-developing phenomenon that it thwarts all hope of the kind of closure that constitutes the very definition of "definition." On the one hand, reflexivity is hardly limited to experimental works. Consider, for example, Georges Rouault's 1916 painting *The Old King*, which does depict a subject's torso and profile but clearly makes no attempt to disguise its brush strokes and pigments. For by so exhibiting the details of its construction, *The Old King* also attends to theoretical considerations, classic questions as to the essence of its media and modes. On the other hand, reflexivity can be found, to some degree, in quite commonplace and popular film and video productions. The revelation of a second camera in television news coverage; the whimsy of a Groucho Marx (in the 1930s) or a Bruce Willis (in the 1980s *Moonlighting* episodes) who deconstruct the fundamental fiction of fictive narrative's invisible camera by looking into the lens to address the audience directly; the employ of academy leader or visible splices in television advertising commercials—all these exemplify reflexivity. Yet the far greater degree of reflexivity—the greater innovation, sophistication, and thoroughness of it in experimental works—suggests a genuine difference in kind. Indeed, so pronounced is this major genre's reflexivity that it constitutes one of the main reasons for much of the misunderstanding (and resulting hostility) surrounding the entire history of experimental production. This misunderstanding is a tedious obstacle for experimental scholars, academics, and artists who often discover themselves wondering why even professional colleagues find endless difficulties in grasping the patent principle that much of the address of such work is precisely the scope and limitations, the contributions and constraints, and the subtle differences and similarities that mainly unite but also separate film and electronic constructions.

While reflexivity is but one of our eight generic characteristics, it can effectively bond the others to reveal experimental motion pictures' unique function as a type of extant, manifest, immediate theory, as direct theory, bypassing the intervention of a separate semiotic system such as the verbal discourse you (the reader) now process and we (the writers) herewith (reflexively) reveal by calling your attention to those marks upon these pages. This final characteristic—reflexivity—will progressively come to dominate the immediate historical overview that follows. There we will see a growing artistic exploration of motion picture essence, an ongoing desire to detect and employ constructions at first independent of literary and dramatic influences and, more recently, the early experimental attachments to painting and music as well.

Poststructural written theory—like deconstruction—is greatly devoted to demonstrating not only the lack of clear textual boundaries but also the related insubstantiality of generic articulation. To be sure, the margins of our proposed major genre of experimental productions can be blurred. First, no one of this chapter's eight characteristics is either necessary for a work's generic inclusion or sufficient for such inclusion. Indeed, a striking variety of configurations from these characteristics—acollaborative construction, economic independence, brevity, technical innovations, mental imagery, avoidance of verbal language, nonnarrative structures, and reflexivity—will manifest in the chapters that follow. Second, a significant number of titles are claimed equally by, for example, the major genre of experimental motion pictures and the major genre of factual motion pictures. Still, the coordinate major genres proposed in this chapter are well supported by contemporary de facto margins. The American Film Institute comparably trichotomized American film and video college curricula. Internationally, countless film and video festivals have employed the fictive, nonfictive, and experimental categories for submission and for prizes. Even grant organizations, like the U.S. National Endowment for the Arts, have employed these margins to provide commonplace categorization for that multifaceted ensemble that we have called motion pictures.[12]

This was not always the case. Before Sheldon Renan published *An Introduction to the American Underground Film*, many personally found it all but impossible to stir up more than the slightest scholastic interest for this curious body of experimental work—so grounded are academic percepts in written texts. Regardless of succeeding texts by Mekas, Curtis, Youngblood, Sitney, Le Grice, and others—and in contradistinction to its coordinate major genres of the nonfiction and the fictive narrative—experimental productions still suffer some serious scholastic neglect. It is hoped that this book's demonstration of that genre's function as direct theory can mitigate this subtle ostracism.

But this major genre began neither with Renan nor with succeeding scholarship. It began rather in the fertile artistic reformation that followed upon the European recovery from World War I. It began, for the most part, in France and Germany with what canonical scholarship has come to call the European avant-garde.

3. The European Avant-Garde

The European avant-garde (EAG) has become a common film history label for that body of experimental production realized by a number of fine artists on the European continent who turned to the cinema as an extension of their work in painting, sculpture, and other media during the decade of the 1920s. In the main, these artists operated in France and Germany under no real organization other than shared concerns with then contemporary artistic movements like cubism, dadaism, futurism, and surrealism.

Partly because of these painterly premises, contemporary motion picture historiography has chosen to differentiate the EAG from a concomitant body of European cinematic innovation equally characterized by a fascination with the powers of editing. This chronologically parallel movement is often termed *Russian formalism* to designate the far more collaborative, industrialized, narrative work of such Soviet filmmakers as Lev Kuleshov, Vsevolod Pudovkin, and the very famous Sergei Eisenstein, whose well-published written theory championed the powers and promises of editing under that term, which he all but invented, *montage.*

Eisenstein's writings were at once explications of his actual production (for example, *Battleship Potemkin* and *October*) as well as prescriptions and proscriptions for future productions. In spite of earlier pioneer efforts in written film theory (Hugo Munsterberg's *The Photoplay: A Psychological Study* and Vachel Lindsay's *The Art of the Moving Picture* were both published in New York City in 1916), one can readily argue that written film theory began with the Russian formalists, especially Eisenstein's early writings—drafted in the final years of the EAG—which are today published under the title *Film Form.*

The diverse address of the *Film Form* essays remains largely devoted to the core theoretical question of medium specificity. That is, what distinguishes and differentiates cinema from other forms, like the novel or theater? While Eisenstein was wont to compare film with Kabuki theater or the novels of Dickens, his contention was that montage's transformational power over time and space provided cinema its most specific, most intrinsic element. Eisenstein repeatedly examined the relationship of such montage to narrative, at times accepting it as a classic storytelling device, at times contending that it rather better served a Joycean stream-of-consciousness, and at times insisting that montage's real essence lay in what he called "intellectual montage," an "intellectual cinema" that would transcend any reliance upon narrativity. Here Eisenstein sought a cinematographic analog to the type of exposition that constituted such philosophic writings as Karl Marx's own *Capital*:

This theory engrossed itself as follows, in transmuting to screen form the abstract concept, the course and halt of concepts and ideas—without intermediary. Without recourse to story, or invented plot, in fact directly—by means of the image-composed elements as filmed. This theory was a broad . . . generalization of a series of possibilities of expression placed at our disposal by the methods of montage and its combinations. The theory of intellectual cinema represented, as it were, a limit, the *reductio ad paradox* of that hypertrophy of the montage concept with which film esthetics were permeated during the emergence of Soviet silent cinematography as a whole and my own work in particular.[1]

However, the EAG's contradistinct approach largely avoided both expository discourse and narrative structures for cinematographic extensions of painting. Few paintings have any real connection with narrative. Narrative depends upon characterization, and the mere appearance of people in a painting or film or lyric poem lacks adequate psychological scope for genuine characterization. Narrative is equally predicated upon a fictive differential, what Christian Metz regards as an *irrealization* derived from diegetic temporal sequence: "A doubly temporal sequence, one must hasten to specify. There is the time of the thing told and the time of the telling (the time of the *significate* [signified] and the time of the *signifier*).["]2 While certain murals, triptychs, and tapestries do realize—in the fashion of the multipaneled cartoon or comic book—narrative characterization and temporality, most painting does not. (Neither, we should add, does it realize the type of exposition that informs the kind of prose that our reader now processes: Eisenstein's intellectual cinema goal.) By the beginning of the EAG, film narrative had already arrived at its contemporary status, being cinema's all-but-exclusive structural characteristic. To be sure, narrative still constitutes cinema's "royal road." The substance of the popular fictive feature that commands our attention at local theaters and that clearly dominates the Academy Awards and even academic attention makes narrative's classic and current prevalence beyond theoretical debate. However, the far more basic, far more substantial theoretical question of whether or not narrative is intrinsic to the cinema is a perennial one that marks the entire corpus of written film theory, from Eisenstein's *Film Form* essays through Metz's *Film Language: A Semiotics of the Cinema*.

Narrative's intrinsic or extrinsic relation to the cinema also marks the entire corpus of the EAG's direct theory. Before we examine this thesis through select EAG works by Fernand Léger, Viking Eggeling, Hans Richter, Man Ray, René Clair, and others, let us first survey some of the pertinent terminology and aesthetic premises of early-twentieth-century art history that can help classify both the cinematic and noncinematic work of the same artists. Appropriately, the following terms—which can also serve as provisional subcategories for our genre of the EAG—have no intrinsic connection to narrative.

Cubism designates an artistic movement that followed upon the work of Paul Cézanne and began by first reconstructing representational images within a framework of Euclidian geometric forms: rectangles, triangles, circles, overlapping planes, and those more solid geometric constructs like the "cubes" from which the movement derived its name. Later work progressively removed itself from such representational qualities for the sake of a pure play of color, line, and cubist form. *Futurism* began with the Italian F. T. Marinetti's "Manifesto" (1909) demanding a doctrinaire veneration of the machine age that progressively surrounded twentieth-century artists and audiences. Sometimes related, *dada* appeared later, flourishing at the very beginning of the EAG. *Dadaism* is characterized by a whimsical rejection of established artistic norms and values with its (oxymoronic) "calculated irrationality" and its emphasis upon chance versus logic or reason. Finally, *surrealism*—which formally began with André Breton's poetic "Manifesto" of 1924—was greatly influenced by Freudian psychology's emphasis upon dreams and the "inner eye," Freud's privileged channels for the unconscious, primary-process communication between id and ego.

Many of the EAG films—being the product of cubist, futurist, dadaist, or surrealist painters—directly fit one or more of these painterly categories. For example, one of the most celebrated and analyzed EAG films is Léger's *Ballet Mécanique* (France, 1924). Modestly collaborative (MGM's Dudley Murphy was cinematographer), *Ballet Mécanique* was independently financed and is rich with such techno-structural devices as split screens, distortion lenses, manic montage, and what is likely the first example of loop printing. This brief experimental work (about fifteen minutes in its "time of the telling") has no real narrative diegesis (that is, Metz's "time of the thing told"), unless one interprets *Ballet Mécanique*'s repeated return to a woman's eyes (the swinging Katherine Murphy at the film's start and finish) as adequate evidence for an interior monologue's stream of consciousness, an intellectual montage constituted by disassociated and associated forms that often echo Léger's cubist/futurist paintings.[3] But what a bizarre stream of consciousness we would find: white circles rapidly intercut with white triangles; the (reflexive) reflections of Murphy and Léger's camera in a sphere; futurist gears or pistons; columns of steel cookware; numbers from signs; animated wine bottles; a carnival ride; a printer-looped hefty female porter who, in a machinelike, precise repetition, reflexively ascends and reascends a stair; an intertitle regarding an expensive *"collier de perles"* (punningly intercut with a leather horse collar); animated mannequin legs; and a white straw hat so rapidly intercut with an oval, white shoe that the threshold between animation's typical use of two or three frame-groups and montage's power to rapidly exchange brief shots is directly deconstructed as the audience experiences a repeated phenomenological metamorphosis between the shoe and the hat.[4]

Anticipating Eisenstein's written theory on editing and its relation to narrative, *Ballet Mécanique* directly plays with the nonnarrative possibilities of montage as well as with the equally pertinent inter-relationships between montage and stream-of-consciousness mentation. But not all EAG production is as varied as *Ballet Mécanique*. For example, about the same year, the Swedish artist Viking Eggeling released another EAG classic, which though also silent bears a musical title: *Symphony Diagonal*. With modest industry support (Germany's UFA studios) but little or no collaboration, and with stunning brevity (just seven minutes long), the animated "diagonal symphony" is, in contrast to *Ballet Mécanique*, totally removed from any hint of narrative. Instead, its design seeks more synaesthetic visual correspondence to musical structures. Its simple, subtle images (see plate 3.1) are too idiosyncratic to be called cubist, but they are remarkably futurist in their recall of the then-new technological phenomenon of neon lighting. *Symphony Diagonal*'s very two-dimensional forms recall the curious quality of neon advertising lights with their mobile abstract patterns typically configured against a night-like blackness. (It is interesting to note that the Frenchman George Claude's invention of neon illumination dates just from the previous decade: 1910.)

Plate 3.1. *Symphony Diagonal* (1924) by Viking Eggeling.

Of course, one need not have actual people for narrative's characterization to manifest. Animals and even objects can possess human psychological attributes by means of anthropomorphism. Yet we believe that no one could discover or even project the hint of anthropomorphic characterization into Eggeling's intricate white forms. *Symphony Diagonal* is quintessentially nonnarrative, having its aesthetic base in the static paintings of the period, which implicitly sought cinema's resource of motion (for example, Marcel Duchamp's *Nude Descending a Staircase* in 1912).

Eggeling constructed *Symphony Diagonal* during an influential friendship with the German artist Hans Richter, whose own *Rhythmus 21* was also animated at the UFA studios. This film's title touches both its year of release (1921) and its synaesthetic design, which silently realizes visual analogs to musical structures. *Rhythmus 21* is quite acollaborative, very brief (about five minutes for its "time of telling"), and incontestably lacking in even the slightest evidence of diegesis—again, Metz's "time of the thing told." Instead, we are faced with a dynamic, cubist exploration of moving rectangles and squares and lines that recall a monochromatic resemblance to earlier and later paintings by the Dutch artist Piet Mondrian. Standish Lawder's insights are appropriate here and suggest implicit reflexivity:

> Richter's first film, *Rhythm 21* [*sic*] was a kinetic composition of rectangular forms of black, grey, and white. Perhaps more than in any other avant-garde film, it uses the movie screen as a direct substitute for the painter's canvas, as a framed rectangular surface on which a kinetic organization of purely plastic forms was composed. For, normally, the movie screen is perceived as a kind of window . . . behind which an illusion of space appears; in *Rhythm 21*, by contrast, it is a planar surface activated by the forms upon it. Thus, its forms, like those of an abstract painting, seem to have no physical extension except on the screen.[5]

The film has neither character nor characterization, and its dynamic patterns preclude even the possibility of anthropomorphism (see plate 3.2). Further, *Rhythmus 21* plays equally well in forward or reverse projection, thereby confounding any hope of establishing a fictive differential. As direct theory, then, *Rhythmus 21* answers the question of cinema's intrinsic or extrinsic connection to narrative several years before Eisenstein's own films and writings and over a half-century before Metz's *Film Language*. Strictly speaking, though, *Rhythmus 21*'s reflexivity depends upon an intertextual regard. Only in comparison and contrast to other, far more popular productions of its period (for example, the early cartoons of Émile Cohl, Winsor McCay, and Randolph Bray; D. W. Griffith's *Broken Blossoms* in 1919; Charlie Chaplin's *The Kid* in 1921) can its historic theoretical address be appreciated.

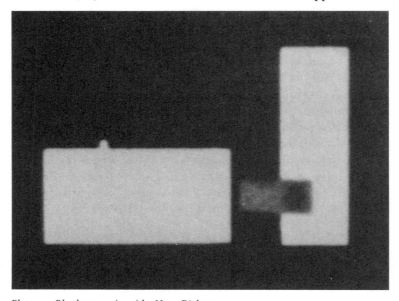

Plate 3.2. *Rhythmus 21* (1921) by Hans Richter.

Ballet Mécanique's reflexivity is less purely intertextual. While no narrative or documentary from its period evidences loop printing, for example, that same loop directly violates audience embrace of diegesis. In watching this EAG film, we are never allowed to reside in a world beyond the screen but are rather abruptly and repeatedly returned to the world of the artifact. *Ballet Mécanique*'s reflexivity insists upon our attendance to the film as film. This strategy depends upon devices in part developed by several dadaists. For instance, Man Ray's later 1923 dadaist film *Retour à la Raison* returns us not to "reason" but to non sequitur. Any hope for an audience to find a diegesis is constantly frustrated by a montage of abstract images intercut with a hanging mobile or moiré patterns projected upon the torso of a nude model.

Ray, the American expatriate photographer who contributed to the EAG in France, devoted his whimsical films to a dadaist deconstruction of narrative hegemony. His delightful "rayograms" directly address medium specificity by realizing images quite independent from the seemingly essential cinematographic apparatus of camera and lenses. The rayograms/rayographs of both *Retour à la Raison* and *Emak Bakia* (1926) may well be the first examples of that highly reflexive form of animation today called "cameraless."[6] Strips of unexposed 35mm motion picture stock were stretched upon a darkroom table and then strewn with such materials as tacks, nails, and confetti. A simple flash of light resulted in random, often high-contrast patterns that became quite lively upon projection. Film is thus directly defined as the (projected) play of abstract or representational images rather than as the result of any camera capture (see plate 3.3).

The EAG was also marked by surrealism, which typically rejected pure abstraction for the sake of cinematographic surrogates of a particular type of mental imagery: dreams. Recall André Breton's doctrinaire insistence upon the surrealist "omnipotence of dreams," following then-popular Freudian premises that the seeming separation between conscious and unconscious was nightly bridged by the id's disguised, censored communication to the ego through dream states. In keeping with these premises, surrealism's oneiric aesthetic aptly excluded abstraction.

René Clair's *Entr'acte* (France, 1924) constitutes an EAG synthesis of both dada and surrealism. With its comic yet fragmented/subverted story, the film retains enough narrativity (including a "character" whom the film follows) to at least raise the question of oneiric verisimilitude. Dreams do have characters—at least that one character of the dreamer. But the dream-character's temporal/spatial transformations transgress the phenomenology of most waking states in addition to the cinematic continuities of most fictive features and many documentaries, which (it could well be argued) stand more as surrogates to our awakened perceptions. For generally, both the fictive and documentary major genres rest their aesthetic upon what

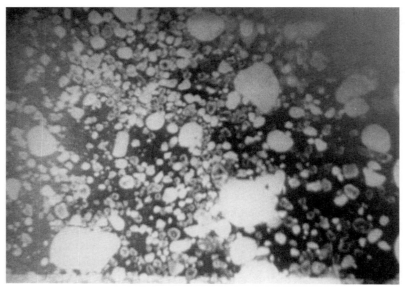

Plate 3.3. *Retour à la Raison* (1923) by Man Ray.

the French theorist André Bazin called the "ontology of the photographic image."[7] From the perspective of this realist/reproductive
written theory, only external phenomena—our consensual realm of
outward perceptions—constitute the proper material of film. Following Bazin, Siegfried Kracauer regarded experimental film's affinity for
interior realms (like dreams) as flying in the face of a "medium which
gravitates toward the veracious representation of the external world."[8]
Entr'acte's representational imagery directly confounds and contradicts
Kracauer's "external world," although it does depend upon a strange
(and often hilarious) narrative. A man at a shooting gallery is himself
shot. His funeral procession (the hearse is pulled by a camel) oneiri-
cally circles a miniature Eiffel Tower before the wheeled-coffin escapes,
beginning a zany chase in which Paris streets metamorphose into roll-
er-coaster hills and which ends with the coffin's corpse, back to life,
reflexively crashing through what appears to be the film's final title: *Fin*.

Even more pronounced in its oneiric transformation of montage's
temporal and spatial powers is the better-known *Un Chien Andalou*
(France, 1929), a bicollaborative surrealist study by the filmmaker
Luis Buñuel and the surrealist painter Salvador Dali. P. Adams Sitney's *Visionary Film* clearly confirms *An Andalusian Dog*'s common
oneiric interpretation:

What Dali and Buñuel achieved through [their] method of com-
piling a scenario was the liberation of their material from the
demands of narrative continuity. Far from being puzzling, the
film achieves the clarity of a dream. The extremity of the vio-
lence and the calculated abruptness of changes of time, place,
and mood intensify the viewing experience without satisfying
the conventional narrative demands of cause and effect. The
concentration on only two actors, male and female, and the
insistence on tactile imagery set up a situation of identification
that more randomly organized films do not have. The strength
of the identification in the context of the abrupt dislocations
and discontinuities provides us with a vivid metaphor for the
dream experience. Had Dali and Buñuel set about to study their
own dreams and clinically re-create a dream on film, they could
not have surpassed *Un Chien Andalou*.[9]

Some examples: a woman exits a door in a city apartment to find herself on a distant beach; a man throws the contents of a suitcase out of an apartment window, in the dead of night, while the reverse shot, from the street, matches the falling garments in broad daylight. Such striking incongruities do attain oneiric verisimilitude. In a more dadaist manner, intertitles (and titles: for the film has nothing to do with either dogs or the Spanish province of Andalusia) defy our expectations for traditional narrative clarification of diegesis. Titles telling us "About three A.M." or "With springtime" confound rather than confirm a temporality already subverted by effects that precede causes (for example, the severed hand of the protagonist). Add to this an admixture of symbols both open to Freudian hermeneutics (as when the protagonist's lust is restrained by a somewhat dadaist tableau of grand pianos, dead moose, and bewildered clergy) and charmingly closed to such interpretation (for example, the recurrent striped box), and we have what may be the EAG's best known though least typical production.

Lesser known are a few EAG realist works that, while corresponding with Kracauer's and Bazin's predication of cinematic essence upon the external world, still warrant inclusion in the avant-garde. Thus, all of the EAG was not antithetic to later written theory that would proscribe abstraction and mental imagery. For example, the Dutch filmmaker Joris Ivens produced the acollaborative, economically independent, brief, nonverbal *Rain* in 1929. The film depicts an afternoon rain shower in Amsterdam and depends upon a quasi-narrative chronology as well as a total divorce from mental images. Indeed, *Rain* is also claimed by the major genre of nonfiction film, although it lacks the political polemics of Ivens's later documentary work. In this fashion, *Rain* could be grouped with a subcategory of films from the period usually called "city symphonies." Such films as Walter Ruttmann's *Berlin* (Germany, 1927) and Alberto Cavalcanti's *Rien que les heures* (France, 1926) join Dziga Vertov's feature-length *Man with a Movie Camera* (Russia, 1929) in being claimed by both historians of the documentary as well as historians of the EAG. These city symphonies straddled the boundary separating the nonfiction and experimental major genres (see figure 3.1), thus providing us another curiosity like the docudramas that questioned and deconstructed the boundary separating the nonfiction and fictive narrative major genres.

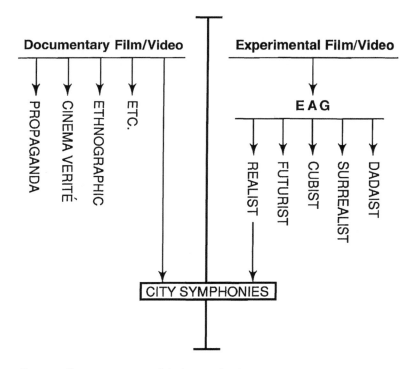

Figure 3.1. European avant-garde's city symphonies.

The retained realism of Ivens's impressionistic sketch of Amsterdam, or the synaesthetic montage portraits of Paris (by Cavalcanti) and Berlin (by Ruttmann), or Vertov's day-in-the-life of a Kino Pravda cinematographer's highly reflexive tour of Moscow (with its bionic comparisons between camera eye and human eye) constitute valuable insights for any revisionist genre theory. These works also reveal a minor realist extension of the EAG beyond its more typical base in such then-current fine arts movements as dadaism, cubism, and surrealism. Sheldon Renan would come to claim *Rain* (which he dates 1928), Cavalcanti's *Nothing but the Hours*, and Ruttmann's *Berlin* as avant-garde classics,[10] while David Curtis calls *Man with a Movie Camera* "something of an avant-garde classic."[11] (Here, Curtis's qualifying "something" is due to the fact that these works also mark such texts as Erik Barnouw's *Documentary*.)[12]

Regardless of the limits of its subcategories, for all practical purposes the EAG came to an end with the international depression
of 1929. This is not to say that certain artists did not continue their
work after 1929. The German-born Oskar Fischinger completed the
prize-winning abstract animation *Composition in Blue* in 1933; this
very cubist and very synaesthetic address of pure form and color
correspondences to precise measures and tones of light classical
music remains a brief, nonnarrative, acollaborative, independent,
nonverbal classic of the late EAG. (But Fischinger fled Germany for
the United States the following year, upon Hitler's Reich Ministry
of Public Enlightenment and Propaganda's sudden prohibition of
"abstraction" in German cinema.)

Recall that a great deal of earlier EAG production was devoted to
synaesthetic questions regarding nonnarrative interrelationships between music and moving images. But whereas *Rhythmus 21, Symphony
Diagonal, Ballet Mécanique*, and the various city symphonies only
implicitly address this aesthetic, Fischinger's *Composition in Blue* is
far more explicit in its investigation. For its construction, Fischinger
analyzed the musical score of Otto Nicolai's overture for the *Merry
Wives of Windsor*, breaking it into units as brief as a sound film's small-
est interval: 1/24 of a second. Next, he employed what appears to be a
somewhat idiosyncratic theory of equivalencies that related Nicolai's
musical tones and metrics to his own animated solid objects (such as
tiny blocks, cylinders, and cubes), cutouts (mainly flat, tear-shaped
forms or varicolored circles), and some cels—all set within a blue box.

Literally, *synaesthesis* means "joint perception" and can involve
any of the senses. A commonplace example would be the aesthetic
crossover from the sense of vision to tactility, as when one regards
rough-hewn sculpture. Phenomenologically, it occurs in various altered states of consciousness, including aesthetic experiences. Charles
Tart's anthology *Altered States of Consciousness* contains a chapter by
Walter N. Pahnke and William A. Richards that details the common
aesthetic interrelationship between music and mental imagery: "If
music is being played, synaesthesia often develops. The [aesthetic]
pattern thus seems to flow with the music, even changing color at
appropriate places."[13]

The psychological phenomenon of synaesthesia clearly marked the written theory of Eisenstein, who (as early as 1928) praised Japanese Kabuki theater because it caused the audience to "actually 'hear movement' and 'see sound.'"[14] Later, Eisenstein was to address the issue of "associating music with color" in his *Film Sense* essay "Synchronization of the Senses." In fact, he labeled "that form of montage" with a neologism: "chromophonic, or color-sound montage."[15]

While a great deal of the EAG's direct theory depended upon dynamic extensions of a painter's canvas, many EAG titles signal an equally musical regard—synaesthetic attempts to somehow relate visual forms, tones, and movements to the type of constructions we rather associate with music. Just as Eisenstein's "metric" and "rhythmic" categories of montage articulated how the "absolute [temporal] lengths" of each film shot intricately interrelated with "the content within the frame,"[16] so too (in a far more direct theoretical fashion) did Richter and Fischinger reveal to us the essentially rhythmic and musical properties of their otherwise nonrepresentational imagery, in a manner aptly termed *synaesthetic.*

These same synaesthetic alternatives to the hegemony of story-cinema help begin experimental motion pictures' quest for constructions that are medium-specific, constructions independent of the narrativity that marks the theater from ancient Greece until the present and marks the novel from its eighteenth-century beginnings through most contemporary best sellers. The privilege of our contemporary vantage reveals that the EAG's function as direct theory perhaps anticipates, perhaps causes later written theory's attacks on both abstraction and mental imagery. (For example, Kracauer's *Theory of Film* essay on the experimental film quietly castigates not only the films and artists of the EAG but later experimental productions as well.) Both concerns—the phenomenology of mental imagery and an exploration of nonnarrative constructions—constitute much of the audience misunderstanding of the EAG not only during the decade of the 1920s but even during our current era. We would here quote Jonas Mekas, one of the best-known apologists for experimental production: "Most people do not like films, they like stories."[17]

Upon its remove to America, experimental production continued to address many of the same questions begun by the EAG. So linked are the European and American bodies of work that the U.S. beginnings are often called the *American avant-garde*, in recognition of these same European influences. However, as the next chapter reveals, the United States was not without provision of indigenous properties as well. Still, we begin with what Sitney posits as "nearly a defining feature" of our major genre—"the rejection of linear narrative."[18]

4. The American Avant-Garde and the American Underground

----

t is convenient to posit a precise end for European avant-garde production with the advent of the Great Depression followed by a sudden
flourish of sometimes fresh, sometimes derivative work in the United
States. Yet certain concomitant productions preclude such consid-
eration. As David Curtis notes, "America's first avant-garde film was
Charles Sheeler's and Paul Strand's *Manhatta*, an isolated attempt
made as early as 1921."[1] Curtis's choice of the qualification "isolated" is,
however, quite telling. Whereas the EAG's body of production is so extensive as to make the titles discussed in chapter 3 but a bare sample,
the American avant-garde (AAG) evidences no comparable largesse.
For the decade of the 1920s, few U.S. experimental productions likely
survive, and only speculation would suggest that future film histories
will eventually reveal many others. In 1928, Robert Florey's *The Life
and Death of 9413—A Hollywood Extra* did provide an experimental
homage to that movement of the fictive feature today called German
cinematic expressionism, but it wasn't until the decade of the 1940s
before we see any real flourish in the AAG.

Among the exceptions to this generalization is, again, Sheeler and
Strand's *Manhatta*. Silent, less than ten minutes long, independently
produced, and distinctly nonnarrative, the film's aesthetic is far more
dependent upon still photography and lyric poetry than upon the
EAG's affinity for painting or musical structures. Indeed, *Manhatta*'s quiet photodocumentary images of New York City are organized
according to passages from a poem by Walt Whitman. Later, in 1929,
the silent H_2O was independently produced by Strand's documentary colleague, the photographer Ralph Steiner. H_2O is a brief (twelve
minute), wordless, acollaborative, independent, highly realist study of

water patterns. Surviving prints retain Steiner's superb photographic skills and structures. The realistic opening shots are progressively replaced by tighter compositions from longer focal-length lenses into a realm of increased "natural" abstraction. Figure and ground become confounded. H_2O's water reflections anticipate computer-generated modulations upon cathode ray tubes that would appear decades later; also, the turbulence and undulations of Steiner's simple subject mimic the strange distortions of fun-house mirrors (see plate 4.1). But all of this is done without EAG recourse to prisms, mirrors, or multiple exposures. In Steiner, the AAG evidences a special, pragmatic respect for what the representationalist written theory of Siegfried Kracauer came to call, three decades later, "the jurisdiction of external reality." Both *Manhatta* and *H_2O* thus constitute exceptions to Kracauer's rule: "[T]he *avant-garde* film makers did not repudiate the hegemony of the story to exchange it for another restrictive imposition—that of the raw material of nature. Rather, they conceived of film as an art medium in the established sense and consequently rejected the jurisdiction of external reality as an unjustified limitation of the artist's creativity, his formative urges."[2] Melding Kracauer's perspective with the often poetic quality of films like *Manhatta* and *H_2O*, we would introduce the label *lyric realism* for this AAG subcategory.

But Kracauer's repeated proscriptions for the avant-garde filmmakers are largely retrospective. Extant written theory of the 1930s (and indeed into the post–World War II period) was the transformationalism of, first, Sergei Eisenstein (along with Vsevolod Pudovkin, Lev Kuleshov, and Béla Balázs), followed by the remarkable popularity of Rudolf Arnheim's essays—written between 1933 and 1938—which are today published under the title *Film as Art.*

Film as Art's written theory depends upon an elaborate, bionic comparison between the cinematographic apparatus and the human sensorium. The text's thesis is designed to repudiate a quoted denigration of cinema: "Film cannot be art, for it does nothing but reproduce reality mechanically."[3] Detailing cinema's "reduction of depth," or then-common "absence of color" and "silence," or the delimitation of the camera's frame, especially the contrast between our real-world phenomenology where "time and space are continuous" versus the power of montage, Arnheim's repeated thesis is clear: "Art

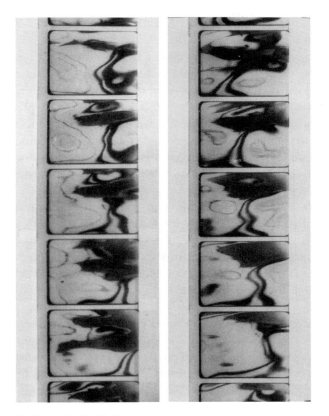

Plate 4.1. *H2O* (1929) by Ralph Steiner.

begins where mechanical reproduction leaves off."[4] Here, Arnheim's position is but an elaboration of the Russian formalists, following Eisenstein, who championed not an aesthetic of reproduction but an aesthetic of transformation.

It is noteworthy that just as we cannot truly truncate the EAG at the year 1929, Arnheim's transformational thesis cannot be limited to the 1930s. Further, *Film as Art* curiously ignores the EAG. Only in isolated instance like his 1957 introduction to these 1930s essays does Arnheim even mention "the remarkable blossoming of the 'abstract' film—the beginnings of what someday will be the great art of painting in motion."[5]

The causal relationships between the written theory of Arnheim and extant AAG productions thus escape assignment. It is far easier to confirm concomitance than to suggest either cause or effect. Again, it is likely that the nature of such concomitance remains intertransformational with written theory and direct theory revealing mutual influences, one upon the other. As we have noted in chapter 1, this highly intertransformational relationship makes systemic reciprocity a far better paradigm than any simple causality. For example, Arnheim's *Film as Art* seems to at once reflect and influence a 1933 AAG production by James Watson and Melville Webber, who are called by Curtis "the first truly avant-garde American film-makers."[6]

Lot in Sodom is a sound film and, probably coincident with the 1933 British translation of Arnheim's *Film als Kunst* into English, deals with the then quite new technological innovation of working sound systems in a manner aptly fitting Arnheim's general rejection of dialogue: "The absence of the spoken word concentrates the spectator's attention more closely on the visible aspect of behavior, and thus the whole event draws particular interest to itself."[7] In this fashion, *Lot in Sodom*'s fifteen-minute-long, fragmented narrative is largely accompanied by music. Its visual construction also confirms Arnheim's transformational emphasis upon such bionic antitheses to "mechanical reproduction" as the employ of multiple exposures, split screens, and prismatic lenses. *Lot in Sodom*'s compounded images so fragment the film's narrative that it alludes to (rather than represents) the biblical account in Genesis (chapter 19). This fragmented quality serves neither dadaist nor surrealist ends, however, in spite of the superimposed imagery that constitutes Lot's prophetic dreams of Sodom's fiery destruction. If *Lot in Sodom* evidences any European influence, it is from German cinematic expressionism's fictive narratives, not the nonnarrative innovations of the EAG. We would therefore introduce the label *expressionist* for this slender subcategory of the American avant-garde genre.

In general, the AAG's varied insistence upon narrative with fragmentation resulted in constructions that reflexively revised the already well-established conventions of Hollywood's classical continuity. For example, Herman Weinberg's silent *Autumn Fire* (1933)—a twenty-minute, independently produced "film poem"—depends upon stream-of-consciousness mental imagery that only hints at the reasons why its mutually enamored hero and heroine are separated. Both the interior monologue and the external mise-en-scénes are quite poetic and remarkably rich in what T. S. Eliot called "objective correlatives" (for example, the woman is repeatedly intercut with soft, quiet trees or flowers at her countryside home, while the man's images are dominated by a harsh, rapid montage of city construction, traffic, and haste). Yet, if *Autumn Fire* is patterned after a poem, it is more narrative—as opposed to lyric—poetry (in contrast to *Manhatta*'s more lyrical, Whitmanesque base). Curiously, Arnheim did not choose to reject narrative in spite of isolated passages in *Film as Art* that seem to bid for nonnarrative possibilities: "It must be admitted that most film directors do not make much original use of the artistic means at their disposal. They do not produce works of art but tell people stories."[8] Likewise, the AAG did not follow the EAG's immediate theoretical rejection of narrative. Rather, the AAG more typically retained a somewhat poetic narrative structure that often directly deconstructed the (by then) internationally established classical continuity conventions it thereby revealed as arbitrary. This indigenous narrative characteristic is particularly pronounced in one especially interesting subcategory of the AAG that was later termed *psychodrama*.

In his 1974 study *Visionary Film*, experimental historian and critic P. Adams Sitney employs the label *American avant-garde* in a fashion far broader than our treatment here. For Sitney, avant-garde covers several decades of American experimental film from early works that followed upon EAG precedents to then-current structuralist productions that constituted the genre's cutting edge at the time of Sitney's publication. Our own taxonomy rather employs AAG as but another, chronologically delimited genre for the major genre of experimental film/video/digital, coordinate with the EAG and subordinating its own subcategories (see figure 4.1).

Figure 4.1's psychodramas are an especially plenteous subcategory of the AAG. These oneiric, fragmented narratives are well analyzed by Sitney's *Visionary Film*, which contends that the "central theme of all the psychodramas that marked the first stage of the American avant-garde cinema is the quest for sexual identity."[9] Sitney also details three other psychodramatic characteristics, namely that psychodramas

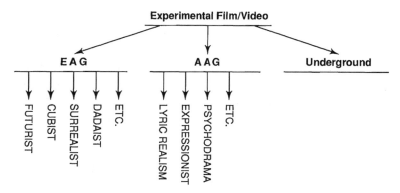

Figure 4.1 American avant-garde.

were a "highly personal psychological drama," that they contained a "strong autobiographical element," and—perhaps most important—that they were "self-acted films" designed to provide the artist with "a process of self-realization."[10]

Maya Deren and Alexander Hammid's *Meshes of the Afternoon* (1943) well exemplifies these characteristics, although Deren's self-acted quest for sexual identity is equally devoted to a concern with death. The narrative begins with Deren's entrance to her home, where she falls asleep. We would point out that Hammid's cinematography and editing for the film's beginning follow classical narrative conventions. Fragmentation, however, follows upon the dream: repeated actions (for example, a key emerging from Deren's mouth); the use of classical continuity's bane—the jump cut—at once retarding and attending Deren's dreamlike ascent to an upstairs bedroom; *Meshes'* montage creating spatial and temporal relationships that defy our waking phenomenology (as when several seemingly continuous steps by Deren shuttle us through several locales). As Sitney attests, oneiric verisimilitude is high: "*Meshes* explicitly simulates the dream experience, first in the transition from waking to sleeping (the shadow covers the eye and the window at the end of the first cycle) and later in the ambiguous scene of waking. The film-makers have observed with accuracy the way in which the events and objects of the day become potent, then transfigured, in dreams as well as the way in which a dreamer may realize that she dreams and may dream that she wakes."[11]

This dreamlike fragmentation of narrative in which the artist personally acts out sexual-psychological problems marks other psychodramas from the AAG period. Curtis Harrington's *Fragment of Seeking* (1946) and Kenneth Anger's *Fireworks* (1947)—though more rudely crafted and far more collaborative in their construction—also depend upon cinematic surrogates for this most common kind of mental image: the dream. Like *Meshes of the Afternoon*, *Fragment* and *Fireworks* were independently produced, are brief (each runs less than twenty minutes), and avoid verbal language (each film's silent actions are set against a simple music background). Homosexuality is the self-revelation for both Harrington and Anger, who self-act their core roles.

With the exception of this then-taboo topic in commercial cinema as well as such narrative fragmentation as jump-cut editing, these otherwise remarkable works provide only modest insights into reflexivity. (As a result, they join lyric realist and expressionist works as somewhat peripheral to our core concern of direct theory.) To be sure, *Meshes*, *Fragments*, and *Fireworks* intertextually reveal as quite arbitrary the certainly well-established forms of Hollywood narrative, but they do so in a manner less thorough than later experimental film/video works that we will examine. In this regard, consider John Hanhardt's American Federation of Arts essay on the American avant-garde film, which clearly addresses reflexivity and implies genuine cinematic discourse: "The avant-garde continues to explore the physical properties of film, and the nature of the perceptual transaction which takes place between viewer and film. It challenges theories of film (such as those of Kracauer and Bazin), which posit as its basis its photographic/illusionistic/representational properties. The traditional coordinates of film/screen/projection are being questioned. . . . The examination of what film is, formally and structurally, is the first step toward ascertaining what film is as a biological/social experience for the viewer."[12]

When this "examination" is reflexively carried out by the films themselves, we have our major function of this major genre: its operation as immediate theory. For all their oneiric accuracy, the psychodramas of the AAG do not fully do this. For clarification of this major function, let us compare an alternate work

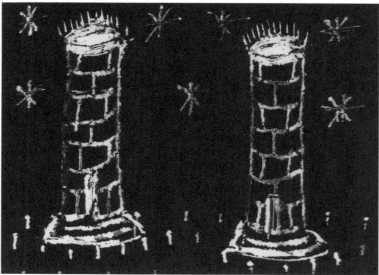

Plate 4.2. *Begone Dull Care* (1949) by Norman McLaren. Courtesy of the National Film Board of Canada.

from the period: Norman McLaren's *Begone Dull Care* (1949; see plate 4.2).

Strictly speaking, *Begone Dull Care* stands outside the genres of the AAG and the American underground because it is a Canadian product. Further, it was a Canadian National Film Board production, which rules out economic independence. However, its brevity, abstraction, absence of verbal language, highly nonnarrative structure, and remarkable technical innovation do provide a pronounced reflexivity that directly explores Hanhardt's "physical properties of film." *Begone Dull Care* is a synaesthetic transformation of its jazz soundtrack (by the Oscar Peterson Quartet) into visual correspondences of color, form, and metrics. Unlike Oskar Fischinger's similar strategies (compare his *Composition in Blue*), McLaren and his collaborator Evelyn Lambert chose the medium of "cameraless animation." Following cameraless experiments by McLaren's British documentary-unit colleague Len Lye, strips of clear and black leader were drawn or scratched upon directly and then edited to match patterns in the soundtrack. Sometimes the procedure was a frame-by-frame matter (in clear keeping with animation's technical basis in single-frame cinematography); sometimes the two artists worked across the frame lines (depending upon the intermittent "single framing" of projection to return the resulting imagery to animation's province). *Begone Dull Care* is quite painterly in that projection. But it does not follow EAG dadaist, surrealist, cubist, or futurist forms. Nor does it follow AAG realist, expressionist, or psychodramatic forms. The film would more accurately be compared to an abstract expressionist painting—in motion.

In its immediate, highly reflexive manner, *Begone Dull Care* examines "what film is, formally and structurally." Directly, the viewer is able to realize that film is neither dependent upon narrative nor upon camera captures of external phenomena. Film is rather the play of (colored) light upon the screen. Also quite directly, *Care* reflexively redefines animation from the concept of cartoon to animation's very stuff and substance, what McLaren himself poetically called "the manipulation of the invisible interstices that lie between the frames." The following quotation was a sign attached to McLaren's animation stand:

The Philosophy Behind This Machine

- Animation is not the art of Drawings-that-move but the art of Movements-that-are-drawn.
- What happens between each frame is much more important than what exists on each frame.
- Animation is therefore the art of manipulating the invisible interstices that lie between frames.[13]

The taxonomic question of just where the AAG ends and where that larger, more varied, and more progressively reflexive genre we have chosen to call *underground* begins defies precise answer. Of course, the revisionist genre theory that informs this entire study repeatedly reveals that all generic articulation is ultimately arbitrary. Whenever one divides a continuum into even two realms, the question of the precise point of boundary arises. From any position well removed from this insubstantial boundary, one can clearly say such-and-such a work (like McLaren's *Begone Dull Care*) is experimental while another work is, for example, documentary. But, as we have seen, a curious number of productions will somehow straddle boundaries and confound clear taxonomic distinction.

Whereas Kenneth Anger's *Fireworks* is probably best categorized as AAG (due to its date as well as its psychodramatic construction), Anger's 1963 *Scorpio Rising* is clearly underground. We employ the label *underground* here in homage to Sheldon Renan's watershed study of 1967—*An Introduction to the American Underground Film.* Although Renan wrote that "the term 'underground film' belongs to the sixties,"[14] its diachronic scope reaches back into the 1950s, while Renan's final chapter, "Expanded Cinema," points ahead to the 1970s—a decade his publication could only (most insightfully) anticipate. Further, for Renan, "underground" was an "inadequate term," in part because many artists themselves "disavow[ed] the word . . . not liking its intimations of seediness and illegality."[15] For our own purposes, these same "intimations" aptly characterize much of the extraordinary flourish of experimental production in the United States during this particular era, when the very distribution of such works often placed them on the level of then illegal pornographic and political productions. Whereas such underground classics as

Stan Brakhage's *Prelude to Dog Star Man* (1961) or Anger's *Scorpio Rising* enjoyed a quite converse aboveground distribution from highly prestigious sources like New York's Museum of Modern Art, during the period from the 1950s into the late 1960s such works had yet to obtain the valuable academic imprimatur that Renan's own 1967 historiography would begin to provide.

This is not to say that all the works Renan cites suffered the ostracism of restricted distribution and limited underground access. For example, Francis Thompson's *N.Y.N.Y.* (1957) received network television broadcast of its surrealist and cubist day-in-the-life portrait of New York City. *N.Y.N.Y.* was neither politically nor artistically problematic, however. Its distortion lenses (in the tradition of the EAG) transformed the city's buildings, traffic, and people, yet did so within a precise chronology that helped assure popular audience appeal.

N.Y.N.Y. constitutes a compendium of Arnheim's transformational menu. Indeed, it could be argued that the entire corpus of American underground work as well as the entire corpus of the AAG (including psychodramas) provide at least modest exemplification of direct theory to the extent that they all embody—in, of course, quite varying degrees—Arnheim's "book of standards."[16] Any intertextual regard will substantiate this argument. Only the rarest documentary or fictive narrative from the period would warrant comparison to AAG and underground innovations. Ferdinand de Saussure's concept of value (as opposed to *meaning*) is not only predicated upon difference but exists in direct proportion to difference; both underground and AAG productions provide a powerful vantage from which more common constructions can be differentially comprehended. Real reflexivity is weak in the films of the AAG and uneven in the films of the underground, yet if Dudley Andrew's interpretation of Arnheim is correct, works like *N.Y.N.Y.* do function as direct theory: "For Arnheim, every medium, when used for artistic purposes, draws attention away from the object which the medium conveys and focuses it on the characteristics of the medium itself."[17] This same reflexive premise is quietly evident throughout the underground work of Stan Brakhage.

Brakhage's career was one of the longest in experimental film, and his productions remain virtually countless. Much of Brakhage's address in these productions is related to his many writings on his concept of vision. In brief, Brakhage's productions and writings both bear out the painter Paul Klee's suggestion that "art does not reproduce what we see, it teaches us how to see."[18] Not many experimental artists also write theory. Hans Richter did, as did Maya Deren, and Norman McLaren's unpublished National Film Board interoffice "memos" are rich in written animation theory. Brakhage's early writings are better known due to a collection published by editor P. Adams Sitney for a special edition of *Film Culture* in 1963 titled *Metaphors on Vision*. The following lines provide capsule insight into this monograph:

> Imagine an eye unruled by man-made laws of perspective, an eye unprejudiced by compositional logic, an eye which does not [logocentrically] respond to the name of everything but which must know each object encountered in life through an adventure in perception.... Suppose the Vision of the saint and the artist to be an increased ability to see—vision. Allow so-called hallucination to enter the realm of perception ... accept dream visions, day-dreams or night-dreams ... even allowing that the abstractions which move so dynamically when closed eyelids are pressed are actually perceived.... There is no need for the mind's eye to be deadened after infancy, yet in these times the development of visual understanding is almost universally forsaken.[19]

To help understand how Brakhage's work functions as direct theory, it is useful to position his writings and films against the 1960 publication of Siegfried Kracauer's highly influential book *Theory of Film*. It is important to come to terms with the rejection of mental imagery that appears in Kracauer's writings and that tends to characterize other members of the realist/reproductive/representational school of written film theory (such as André Bazin). The reason for the rejection lies deep within Kracauer's tautologic equation of reality per se with what he terms "camera reality."[20] Kracauer's position espouses the behaviorist psychology that had been academically established by the time of both his and Brakhage's writings, a psychology that began by admitting the difficulty of examining mental images and ended by denying the very existence of such activity.

In contrast, early psychology (for example, Francis Galton, William James, Sigmund Freud, Carl Jung) was devoted to the phenomenology of mental imagery. Further, post-behaviorist psychology cataloged a great variety of mental images. By definition, mental images are perceptions without external stimuli with the exception of such stimulus agents as drugs, hypnotic commands, or pressure on the eye itself. For contemporary Western cognitive and perceptual psychology, such a catalog would contain afterimages, hallucinations, dreams, memory (and eidetic) images, thought images, hypnopompic/hypnagogic (that is, post-waking/pre-dream) images, and entoptic images (closed-eye percepts of "floaters," actual optic debris). We should be struck by the synchronicity of *Metaphors on Vision* and Robert Holt's watershed article, "Imagery: The Return of the Ostracized" (1964), which heralded scores of later scientific writings on mental images (by cognitive psychologists like Robert Holt, Alexandra Horowitz, P. W. Sheehan, Ulric Neisser, Gabriel M. A. Segal, B. R. Bugelski, Jennifer C. Richardson, and S. Jay Samuels).[21]

Currently, such scholars and research tend to collect under an intrinsically interdisciplinary movement called *cognitive science*, which bonds cognitive psychology with philosophy, artificial intelligence, linguistics, and so on.[22] While cognitivism's interdisciplinarity is not an open set, several film theorists have begun to employ its empirical insights in their own research. For example, William C. Wees's 1992 book, *Light Moving in Time*, is implicitly cognitive in its address of the "visual aesthetics of avant-garde film." We find Wees's discussion of Brakhage most sophisticated:

In his campaign to give "eye's-mind a chance," Brakhage has confronted two major obstacles. The first is the cultural bias that not only separates thinking from seeing but relegates seeing to a secondary or supporting role in the drama of mental life. As Brakhage has put it, "We don't know how to let the eyes think, or how to be conscious of eye-thought." The second obstacle is a consequence of the first: viewers of his films, including many critics, seem to have great difficulty equating the imagery of the films with the phenomena of actual visual perception. This difficulty was exemplified for Brakhage when, as he describes it, P. Adams Sitney "refus[ed] to close his eyes and see if he couldn't see something that was related to the painting on my film." Though one of Brakhage's most insightful and sympathetic critics, Sitney seemed unwilling to grant the possibility that the sources for certain aesthetic effects in Brakhage's films might be found behind his own closed eyelids.[23]

Brakhage's *Prelude to Dog Star Man* is a direct catalog of such mental imagery. Just under thirty minutes long, *Prelude* begins in both blackness and silence. (Typical of most of Brakhage's devotion to vision in his works, the silence is retained throughout.) The blackness is repeatedly interspersed with striking surrogates for Brakhage's aesthetic phenomenology of his closed-eye vision. Some images are like dreams (indeed, Brakhage himself "reads" *Prelude* as dreamlike); others have the ephemeral clarity of hypnagogic imagery (that is, mental images, usually brief and rapidly replaced, that preface the actual dream state). Employing cameraless constructions, distortion lenses, and super-impositions; rushing from macroshots of snow to cosmic shots of the sun to brief memory-like images of lovemaking; rich with abstractions that paradoxically play at the representation of stimulated optic-nerve patterns or entoptic "floaters," *Prelude* quietly mounts image upon image, blackness to pure color to distorted representations, without any dependence upon narrative's popular appeal.

Further, within a major genre marked by acollaborative quintessential auteurism, Brakhage has become a hallmark. All funding, conception, scripting (although Brakhage really did not use scripts in the usual sense of the term), cinematography, editing, lighting, direction, and even (at times) acting come from Brakhage's eye and hand. Removed from the demands of industrial economics, living in almost monastic seclusion with his wife and children, Brakhage devoted a great deal of his production since the early underground era to the construction of surrogates—cinematographic simulacra—for the insubstantial images found behind closed eyes: mental images. In presenting those constructs, films like *Prelude* directly contradict and confound the written theory of realists like Kracauer and Bazin while confirming cognitivism's contemporary interest in mental imagery.

Another classic underground production of the period, Kenneth Anger's *Scorpio Rising*, also directly contradicts realist proscription.

Recall that Bazin's writings castigated not so much montage per se as a certain type of montage that produced

> the creation of a sense or meaning not proper to the images themselves but derived exclusively from their juxtaposition. . . . Finally there is "montage by attraction," the creation of S. M. Eisenstein . . . which may be roughly defined as the reinforcing of the meaning of one image by association with another image not necessarily part of the same episode—for example the fireworks display in *The General Line* following the image of the bull. In this extreme form, montage by attraction was rarely used even by its creator but one may consider as very near to it in principle the more commonly used ellipsis, comparison, or metaphor.[24]

Again, Eisenstein himself called this kind of editing *intellectual montage*, and as Bazin suggests, its form is typically that of the trope. For instance, in Eisenstein's feature narrative *October* (1928), images that are not established in the film's diegesis are interpolated for the cinematographic analog of metaphor. Eisenstein's own examples in his written theory on *October* focus upon the edited comparisons between the diegetically established characters Kornilov and Kerensky with various nondiegetic images of primitive and modern deities: the famous "Gods Sequence." Eisenstein, as early as 1929, was quick to point out that such "rarely used" experiments toward "a kind of filmic reasoning . . . were very much opposed by the majority of critics."[25] (Indeed, their explicit rejection under the Soviet Socialist realism that came into fashion with the 1930s is doubtless the reason why intellectual montage is absent from Eisenstein's later films while so pronounced in its relegation to his later writings.) Intellectual montage, however, came to dominate Anger's *Scorpio Rising*, three decades later.

Scorpio Rising depends upon a fragmented narrative featuring the unnamed protagonist, whom critics usually call "Scorpio." In part, this underground film is a quasi-documentary sketch of motorcycle gangs in both New York and California, many of whom are involved in (at times quite explicit) homosexual activities. This diegetic base allows Scorpio to become the tenor for a multiplicity of metaphoric vehicles by means of an elaborate intellectual montage. (If the results

are a simile, they bear the complexities of an epic simile or of Eliza-
bethan and metaphysical conceits.) The stereotypic image of the late-
1950s/early-1960s biker is at once interwoven with homosexual orgies,
nondiegetic compilation footage of Jesus Christ (from a then-popular
television series), and Nazi inserts (for example, Hitler). Each systemic
vehicle reciprocally informs the others to serve the tenor—Scorpio—
in a manner that is not only sacrilegious but fascist and obscene
as well. Set to thirteen rock-and-roll songs, *Scorpio Rising* became
prototype for the 1969 popular feature *Easy Rider* (providing a good
example of experimental film/video's "laboratory function," which we
will examine below). But its complex employ of intellectual montage
constitutes an equally striking example of direct theory, virtually
defying Bazin's (then yet to be translated) attacks on montage as "that
abstract creator of meaning."[26] Further, Anger's employ is not merely
an extension of Eisenstein's own experiments with intellectual montage in *October*. For in *October*, Eisenstein's nondiegetic materials
were—like the much larger diegetic body of the film—shot under his
direction by his cinematographer, E. Tisse. A great deal of Anger's
nondiegetic material, in contrast, was compilation footage—material
constructed by typically anonymous people for vastly diverse purposes. In fact, Anger's very lack of homogeneity, of seamlessness at
the junction of each interpolation, reflexively reveals this device of
compilation while providing a great deal of the "shock" that Eisenstein
had predicted would always be in direct proportion to the variable
power of intellectual montage's future employ.

Compilation is a transgeneric technique. Typically, its use in other
genres (for example, a Hollywood feature on the Hindenburg disaster
or Frank Capra's *Why We Fight* documentary series during World
War II) is dependent upon an editor's ability to disguise (as much
as possible) any sense of interpolation. Lens resolution, stock grain,
and matters of tonality, style, composition, exposure, and so on—all
can call attention to compilation materials. In this fashion, the typical compilation editor's task is akin to a tailor's who seeks to repair
("French-weave") a hole in a fine garment. Eisenstein's *October* has an
intrinsically seamless quality for its intellectual montage. But Anger
intuitively follows the earlier Russian formalist Viktor Shklovsky's
notion of "baring-the-device," of calling audience attention to the

compilation by reflexively revealing interpolated emulsions—thereby making *Scorpio Rising* almost as much a film about the powers of montage as it is a film about homosexual bikers.

It is difficult to believe that Anger was unaffected, in his reflexive compilation, by the highly popular work of another major figure in the American underground: Bruce Conner. Conner's even more reflexive and far more pervasive body of compilation films marked such early productions as *A Movie* (1958). Running a dozen minutes, technically innovative in its almost total compilation (only the film's reflexively repeated titles were shot by Conner), economically independent in its assemblage of found footage, nonnarrative in its myriad intellectual montage juxtapositions that suggest the often bizarre associations of mental imagery, and set to a musical score that avoids verbal language, Conner's highly reflexive *A Movie* does raise questions regarding the remaining generic characteristic of acollaborative construction. The various shots that Conner's montage has bonded together were taken from scores of different sources: old Hollywood features, old pornographic movies, newsreels, various kinds of leader (for example, after a few minutes into *A Movie*, we read the projectionist title "End of Part Four"), and various documentaries. Thus, only by realizing that this is an "editor's film" can we conclude that Conner himself is clearly the quintessential auteur. Just as a modern sculptor might seek an automobile bumper from a junkyard to provide a unit for his welded construction yet need never credit Ford or General Motors for his completed art object, so too does Conner's use of found footage never really negate our characteristic of acollaborative construction.

Conner's career was very long, and, with few exceptions, his many films fully depend upon compilation for their aesthetic. Typically, he plays his compiled images against musical soundtracks (though his 1967 *Report*, which deals with the 1963 assassination of JFK, is richly reflexive in its often ironic, often caustic contrapuntal juxtaposition of compiled images against the equally found object of the film's narration—taken from radio broadcast material on the day of the Dallas shooting). In several cases, Conner's musical choices have been popular music, and works like *Cosmic Ray* (1961, to Ray Charles's "What Did I Say?"), *Permian Strata* (1969, to Bob Dylan's "Rainy Day Women #12 and #35"), and *Mongoloid* (1978, to the song "Mongoloid" by Devo) constitute fine examples of experimental film/video's (somewhat secondary) function as a laboratory for more popular (and far more economically successful) fare. While each of these three compilation works preceded "music videos," they are clear prototypes for the form; indeed, a remarkable percentage of videos shown on early MTV employed compilation.[27]

From the perspective of reflexivity, Conner's earlier works more clearly exhibit Shklovsky's concept of "baring-the-device." *A Movie*, *Cosmic Ray*, and *Report* make little attempt to match emulsions or to disguise the distinct tones, compositions, and resolutions resulting from distinct cinematographers, stocks, and lenses. Again, Eisenstein predicated intellectual montage's directly discursive power upon its shock. That is, such nonnarrative, often tropic montage powers were in direct proportion to their very nondiegetic sense of interpolation. Early Conner productions capitalize upon such disparity. We are constantly reminded that we are watching not only a movie but a very synthetic movie that rarely depends upon more typical invisible editing. In contrast, later Conner, such as his 1976 *Crossroads* (compiled from declassified Bikini bomb footage), is far slower paced and far less interpolative in montage juxtapositions. Likewise, Conner's 1977 *Take the 5:10 to Dreamland* in fact employs sepia-toned prints to essentially "homogenize" potential disparity. The result is a distinctly quieter mood and a somewhat mitigated reflexivity.

While Conner's compilations, early or late, attend to a variety of subjects, such as sexuality (*Cosmic Ray*), the combined zany antics and genuine horror of contemporary civilization (*A Movie*), the sacrificial death of a beloved president (*Report*), the paradoxical power of atomic weapons (*Crossroads*), or visualized rock music (*Permian Strata*), ultimately his real, reflexive subject always remains montage itself. While one can read the written theory of Eisenstein or Kuleshov or Dziga Vertov for insights into and elaborations upon the intrinsically filmic (and, later, video) resource of montage, one can also screen *A Movie* or *Report* and glean comparable—but always distinct—theoretical insights. Moreover, it might well be argued that Conner continued to produce precisely the kind of films that Eisenstein's written theory predicted and prescribed—films that Eisenstein was unable to construct due to political pressures. So pronounced is Conner's reflexivity, so thorough is his compilation, that both his early works like *Cosmic Ray* and his later sepia-toned compilations like *Valse Triste* (1979) do more than merely complement extant written theory. By their directness, by their insistence upon addressing montage with montage, they transcend the limitations of written theory. Eisenstein's *Film Form* is rich in written discourse on montage, but it can never *be* montage; written words depend upon a very distinct semiotic system when compared to edited images. *A Movie* employs few words (and those humorously, reflexively), but it directly, immediately displays and evidences—literally (due to the very juncture of the splices themselves) articulates—what Eisenstein was verbally trying to point to, trying to indicate when he wrote in *Film Form* that in montage, "degree of incongruence determines intensity of impression."[28]

Plate 4.3 exemplifies one of *Cosmic Ray's* highly incongruent intellectual montage juxtapositions. A shot of a missile that looks like a V-2 rocket is followed by a shot of a naked woman riding a witchlike broom. Two of Conner's "themes" in *A Movie* (war/weapons/death and sexuality) are also united here not by narrative diegesis but by intellectual montage's commonplace ploy of formal similarities/differences. Against contrasting light and dark backgrounds, the diagonal vectors and identical screen direction help to formally underscore this strange trope.

The American underground film boasts countless artists whom our highly selective survey must overlook. Renan's *Introduction to the American Underground Film* contains "A Gallery of Film-Makers," most of whom have been bypassed by this chapter: Bruce Baillie, Robert Breer, Tony Conrad, and Jordan Belson will be addressed in chapter 5, but Carmen D'Avino, Ed Emshwiller, Ken Jacobs, Larry Jordan, Stanton Kaye, the Kuchar brothers, George Landow, Gregory Markopoulos, Jonas Mekas (whose diary-folk films characterize an especially interesting subcategory),[29] Marie Menken, Robert Nelson, Ron Rice, Harry Smith, Stan Vanderbeek, and Jack Smith remain for other studies. (These studies could also provide finer articulation of subcategories for the underground beyond Brakhage's closed-eye vision surrogates, Thompson's neo-cubist/surrealism, Mekas's diaries, McLaren's cameraless—and almost always abstract—expressionism, and the compilations of Anger and Conner.) Many of our overlooked

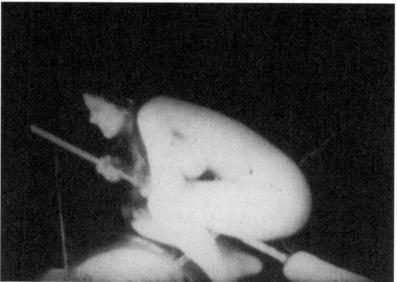

Plate 4.3. *Cosmic Ray* (1961) by Bruce Conner.

artists were highly reflexive in their constructions. To quote Renan: "The films were self-consciously *film*. As in modern art, the materials and the processes of making the work of art (the grain, the scratching on film, the mid-frame splices, the shaky camera) became part of the work of art. The film-makers were not interested in creating a fictional reality for the camera to record objectively. Primarily they wanted to manipulate reality with camera and editing and to produce thereby a different [reality], a film reality that had a sense of being film."[30]

However, a great deal of experimental production began to take new directions with the advent of the new decade of the 1970s. These directions were also marked by an ever-increasing reflexivity and resulting theoretical address. While Conner's compilations are exemplary direct theory, his reflexivity in that compilation still shares center stage with his subject matter. Only with later (and also concomitant) structuralist work does reflexivity so dominate construction that whatever other subjects might manifest become impertinent, become but a means to a much more purely theoretical end.

5. Expanded Cinema and Visionary Film

Sheldon Renan's pioneer study concludes with a chapter anticipating a "whole new area of film and film-like art . . . *expanded cinema*."[1] Approximately three years later, Gene Youngblood's book *Expanded Cinema* continued documentation of the explosive growth of experimental motion pictures' affinity for technologic innovations: "If one considers the introduction of sound then color as successive 'generations' in the history of cinema, it is possible to say that we've entered the fourth generation by marrying basic cinematic techniques to computer and video sciences. There have been no fundamental breakthroughs in the nature of cinema since its conception. In one sense the history of film is but a footnote to Lumière and Méliès. But the technological revolution begins the new age of cinema."[2]

As Youngblood maintains when discussing the complex, pyrotechnic printer films of Pat O'Neill, "New tools generate new images."[3] That is to say, *Expanded Cinema*'s special attention to the confluence of cinema's mechanical-chemical properties and to those far more electronic properties dependent upon video and computers is at once part and parcel of experimental motion pictures' characteristic affinity for increased technological innovation. It also continues an inextricably interrelated devotion to constructions beyond the bounds of most cinema's somewhat parasitic relation to narrative. To help clarify this insight that changes and exchanges of technology (or "techniques") are inseparable from structural changes, and are thereby extraordinarily consequential, Small fashioned a neologism—*technostructure*. More, this term is based upon the distinct historiography of the man to whom this revised edition is dedicated: Raymond Fielding. As we will clarify in our final chapter, Fielding's extensive body of publications realized discussion in a 1985 book by Robert C.

Allen and Douglas Gomery: *Film History: Theory and Practice*. In their preface, they state, "We recognize that film is and has been a multifaceted phenomenon: art form, economic institution, cultural product, and technology. Traditionally, each of these facets has been treated as a separate subdiscipline in film history. In recognition of this fact, we have divided our discussion of film historical research into aesthetic, technological, economic, and social chapters. Although this is certainly not the only division that could have been made, it does represent the major lines of film historical research to date and provides a useful way of grouping the [methodologies]."[4]

Fielding virtually constitutes Allen and Gomery's leading example of what they term *technological determinism*. By coupling it with Ferdinand de Saussure's revolutionary concepts of semiotics, Small's technostructure helps distinguish this coupling from Fielding's groundbreaking historiography.

If structure is the interrelationship of the parts to the whole, there are serious theoretical problems attendant upon the quite typical reduction of technique and technology to adjunct phenomena that serve the structure of a work yet are themselves somehow outside that structure. (Recall the fundamental structuralism of Saussure's regard for the gestalt unity of signifier and signified in the operation of any sign system.) Pat O'Neill's *7362* (1965–67) is so reflexively interwoven with the technology of step-optical printers (the film's very title is a stock emulsion number) that the resulting images are not merely pre-electronic, lavishly colored extensions of European avant-garde abstraction. Rather, O'Neill's immediate and quite theoretical address is the typically overlooked possibilities of step-optical printers, which often serve only comparatively pedestrian functions, such as creating freeze frames in fictive features or reducing 70mm and 35mm features into a more commonplace 16mm format. In direct contrast, *7362* exhibits the step aspect of the printer as a kind of animation device that not only allows rapid exchanges of colors but a remarkable control of motion, while the optical aspect allows kaleidoscopic symmetries and configurations of barely representational images (for example, oil pumps and human dancers). *7362*'s reflexivity is technostructural.

O'Neill's later *Runs Good* (1969–70) has far more representational imagery and stands as a step-optical printer study of the kind of compilation we associate with Bruce Conner. With its title charm-ingly reminiscent of a simple used-car ad, *Runs Good* begins with the staccato step printing of a drive through a tunnel, yielding to a delightful, dadaist montage of academy leader and storm footage, yielding to found footage (almost home movie in quality) of a mul-tiple wedding—all to a soundtrack of music and effects. The sound is then replaced by narration from a period documentary ("Wherever they go in India, our boys will see tricks of magic") while O'Neill's contrapuntal imagery optically maintains two frames—an exterior frame of looped, high-contrast, big-game hunting footage and a rectangular interior frame of a magician's hands doing a card trick. The film's twenty-minute running time continues such multilayered, lavishly colored or contrasted imagery combined with dadaist non sequitur (often looped and serial) progressions. To make sense of it, one must return to the etymology of both *sense* and *aesthetic* (a study of sense/perception); the audience must abandon the insulation of hermeneutics as well as the hope for a story; the viewers must return to their direct senses of sight and sound to witness a dazzling theo-retical "articulation" of many of the step-optical printer's overlooked technostructural resources.

Youngblood came to label O'Neill's work *kinesthetic cinema*, in-sightfully calling attention to its function as a kind of nonverbal, ineffable theory: "The dynamic interaction of formal proportions in kinesthetic cinema evokes cognition in the inarticulate conscious. . . . In perceiving kinetic activity the mind's eye makes its empa-thy-drawing, translating the graphics into emotional-psychological equivalents meaningful to the viewer, albeit meaning of an inartic-ulate nature. 'Articulation' of this experience occurs in the percep-tion of it and is wholly nonverbal."[5] However, it is within the even more immediate dyadic articulation of film's mechanical-chem-ical properties and video's far more electronic properties, which Youngblood calls *videographic*, that we find *Expanded Cinema*'s most insightful address of experimental film/video's direct theory during this period.

The cover of *Expanded Cinema* is a frame from Scott Bartlett's *OFFON* (1967), "whose existence was equally the result of cinema and video disciplines":

Like all true videographic cinema, *OFFON* is not filmed TV, in the way that most movies are filmed theatre. Rather it's a metamorphosis of technologies. . . . What happens in *OFFON* is extraordinary. The basic source of video information was in the form of twenty film loops . . . culled from more than two-hundred loops . . . made for a multiprojection light concert. . . . Black-and-white loops were fed through a color film chain in [a] television control room, adding videotronic phosphor-texture to the cinematic graphics. Simultaneously, other loops and portions of Glen McKay's light show were rear-projected onto a screen on the studio floor, which was televised as a second video source. Both video sources were routed into one monitor. . . . A second TV camera televised the monitor, feeding the signal to a videotape recorder. This master tape was again processed through the switching/mixing system . . . [while] a special camera was set up in front of a monitor that filmed at a video rate of 30 fps instead of the movie rate of 24 fps.[6]

Thus, Bartlett's original mechanical-chemical images were first transferred to video formats for superimposures, electronic mattes, and repolarization into negative or high contrast composites, and they were then provided an electronic regress through video feedback (where a camera records its own monitor), given symmetrical bifurcations, and so on. These same electronic constructions were again returned to film's mechanical-chemical format, where sound, editing, and color were added. *OFFON* was released as a 16mm film, but it is neither film nor video—it is rather an often subtle, more often highly reflexive confluence of the two modes that directly articulates both similarities and differences in a manner far more immediate (and far more precise) than any written description of the work's technostructure.

Small personally prefers his own term *cinevideo* to describe and categorize works like *OFFON*. Cinevideo embodies two interrelated denotations: first, it serves to label extant constructions like *OFFON* that are neither film nor video but rather a complex, synergetic interweaving of the two forms; second, cinevideo can help call attention to that larger, ongoing confluence that reciprocally reforms both cinema and television. Cinevideo can help us directly understand that film and video are really quite similar when compared and contrasted to either narrative or nonnarrative constructions—such as the novel or short story (fictive prose narratives) and theatrical narratives (plays, drama), let alone sculpture or painting or music—that rely upon other semiotic systems. As Roland Barthes declared, "Structure depends upon the material used."[7] And in contrast to the materials of written language, dramatic spectacle, and paint and canvas, the technostructural similarities between mechanical-chemical and electronic constructions of moving images are as equally interesting and instructive as their differences. (This same insight will come to flourish in our next chapter on experimental video.)

Not all the works that Youngblood's *Expanded Cinema* documents are products of either step printers or cinevideo. Harkening back to what Renan had called the West Coast Optical School, Youngblood also details such highly influential works as James Whitney's *Yantra* (see plate 5.1), "an inspired and arduous project, which was to consume ten years before its completion. Drawn entirely by hand on small filing cards, it was an attempt to relate images to yoga experiences."[8] Completed in 1957 and less than ten minutes long, *Yantra* is questionably cataloged as abstract. Witness Stan Brakhage's concept of closed-eye

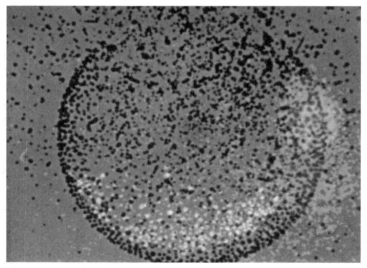

Plate 5.1. *Yantra* (1957) by James Whitney.

vision and our generic attribute of experimental film/video's affinity for mental imagery. Distinct from Western psychology's panoply of mental images, however, *Yantra* attends to an Asian phenomenology related to Hindu and Buddhist philosophy/religion/psychology (three Occidental terms that are intrinsically amalgamated within more Oriental articulation). As Youngblood asserts in his preface, "When we say expanded cinema we actually mean expanded consciousness."[9]

A yantra is a visual meditative device; in a sense it is a memorized mandala, those ubiquitous, archetypal images that so fascinated Carl Jung:

> The Sanskrit word *mandala* means "circle" in the ordinary sense of the word. In the sphere of religious practice and in psychology it denotes circular images which are drawn, painted, modeled, or danced. . . . As psychological phenomena they appear spontaneously in dreams, in certain states of conflict, and in cases of schizophrenia. Very frequently they contain a quaternity or a multiple of four, in the form of a cross, a star, a square, an octagon, etc. . . . In Tibetan Buddhism the figure has the significance of a ritual instrument (*yantra*), whose purpose is to assist meditation and concentration.[10]

An extraordinary percentage of expanded cinema—which here denotes a specific genre of experimental works—evidences mandala structures, what Jung called the *"archetype of wholeness."*[11] *OFFON*, for example, contains a great deal of highly reflexive video feedback (where a video camera is pointed at its own monitor to achieve a seemingly infinite electronic regress of images); by canting the camera forty-five degrees, mandala images are created, a curious techno-structural artifact intrinsically and reflexively related to the video circuitry. Likewise, Jordan Belson's *Allures* (1961) fills its nine minutes of projection with a diversity of mandala structures.

Belson's methods of construction are not reflexive in the way that *OFFON*'s constructions are. Whereas Bartlett is wont to reveal the potentially seamless boundary of his CRT displays, Belson's far more subtly mixed employ of oscilloscopes, step printers, animation, and real-time cinematographic captures of rotating mandalic forms tends rather to disguise his methods. *Allures'* reflexivity is, instead, intertextual; it exists in contradistinction to the comparable absence of these otherwise omni-present, archetypal forms in not only fictive features and documentaries but even other genres of experimental film/video.

It is again difficult to call such imagery "abstract" for the same reasons that it would be difficult to call the seemingly nonrepresentational imagery of Brakhage's *Prelude to Dog Star Man* abstract. "I first have to see the images somewhere," Belson says, "within or without or somewhere. I mean I don't make them up."[12] Further, such quite esoteric works as *OFFON* or *Yantra* or *Allures* are not without evidence of experimental motion pictures' laboratory function. Countless classic (computer-generated) television logos are directly or indirectly derivative for their far more commercial function. Indeed, Douglas Trumbull's commercial success with *2001*'s "stargate sequence" had "precedent in the work of John Whitney."[13]

In the main, our genre of expanded cinema designates West Coast productions of the late 1960s and early 1970s. Predicated upon such complex technostructural resources as step-optical printers, computers, and video's fluent electronic capabilities for transforming the basic realism of photographic or videographic images, expanded cinema is easily characterized by its very complexity. Montage, for example, is often manic in its pace (though expanded cinema's complex cutting is often also mitigated by electronic or mechanical metamorphoses where one image blends into another, within the parameters of topologic similarities). Color is drawn from a vast palette of pure (filter) tones that recall the aesthetic of neon advertising lights. Music is typically synthetic (that is, electronically distinct from instrumentation based upon Newtonian physics such as strings). Superimpositions and mechanical or electronic mattes allow subtle, surreal juxtapositions of representational and abstract imagery, often so multilayered that all sense of figure and ground is abandoned for an aesthetic of collage. So extremely transformational is expanded cinema that—over four decades later—it provides substantiation of Rudolf Arnheim's visionary prediction for an "exclusive film," based upon his transformational premise that "because the potentialities within an art medium create the urge to use them, whimsical, fantastic products will appear, compared with which the wildest futurism of the twenties will seem like innocuous ornaments."[14]

At roughly the same time as expanded cinema's flourish, however, the East Coast of the United States was developing a converse aesthetic, typically closer to André Bazin's representational premise that "the cinema is objectivity in time."[15] More directly, this very minimalist movement, which P. Adams Sitney came to call "structural film" (in chapter 12 of *Visionary Film*), is not unrelated to the post-Bazinian written theory that began to manifest in America during the early 1970s under the then-arcane titles *semiotics* and *structuralism*. Our (transient) geographic dichotomy is not without countless exceptions. For example, Youngblood's *Expanded Cinema* devotes several pages and plates to Michael Snow's 1967 *Wavelength*, "the forerunner of what might be called a Constructivist or Structuralist school of cinema, including . . . at least two of Bruce Baillie's films, *All My Life* and *Still Life* [both 1966],"[16] while Sitney's *Visionary Film* also discusses these two Baillie "versions of the structural film."[17]

In fact, Sitney's *Visionary Film* embodies so many historical periods —from the EAG through psychodrama and Brakhage's underground work into expanded cinema—that his title (unlike Youngblood's) will not serve to help characterize any single genre of experimental motion pictures. However, Sitney's core theoretical essay, "Structural Film," which at once defined and anticipated then-contemporary painting's "minimalist" influence upon our major genre, does demand such reference. While we personally prefer our own composite term *minimalist-structuralist* to identify this body of work, clearly Sitney's publication came to realize a combined descriptive and prescriptive influence not only upon the largely East Coast artists like Snow whom he addressed but also the later West Coast and eventual international extension of the structural aesthetic.[18]

Sitney's *Visionary Film* saw this structural aesthetic as having as "major precursor" the painter/filmmaker Andy Warhol, whose insistence upon fixed-frame, long takes suggested at least one of Sitney's own characteristics for the structural film: "Four characteristics of the structural film are its fixed camera position (fixed frame from the viewer's perspective), the flicker effect, loop-printing, and rephotography off the screen. Very seldom will one find all four characteristics in a single film, and there are structural films which modify these usual elements."[19] As we shall see, each of these four (categorical) characteristics possesses great potential for reflexivity, returning audience members' awareness to the very technostructure of the artifact they behold. Indeed, Sitney contends that these works constitute "a cinema of structure in which the shape of the whole film is predetermined and simplified, and it is that shape which is the primal impression of the film."[20]

From the privileged perspective of hindsight, the advent of Snow's watershed work *Wavelength* in 1967 seems synchronically interrelated with Hugh Gray's 1967 English translation of Bazin's first volume of *What Is Cinema?* Even today, *What Is Cinema?* remains one of the most influential classic written theories, perhaps second only to Sergei Eisenstein's *Film Form* essays on montage, which provided Bazin a fine foil for his later, revisionist regard of cinema's essence. Again, in designed contrast to Eisenstein's essential respect for the transformational power of editing, Bazin's representationalism rather championed a cinema of duration. Further, Bazin's well-developed theorizing upon the intrinsic merit of the long take—"real time, in which things exist, along with the duration of the action for which classical editing had insidiously substituted mental and abstract time"—is interrelated with Bazin's three aesthetic consequences of depth of field[21]:

1. That depth of focus brings the spectator into a relation with the image closer to that which he enjoys with reality. Therefore, it is correct to say that, independently of the contents of the image, its structure is more realistic;

2. That it implies, consequently, both a more active mental attitude on the part of the spectator and a more positive contribution on his part to the action in progress. While analytical montage only calls for him to follow his guide, to let his attention follow along smoothly with that of the director who will choose what he should see, here he is called upon to exercise at least a minimum of personal choice. It is from his attention and his will that the meaning of the image in part derives;

3. From the two preceding propositions, which belong to the realm of psychology, there follows a third, which may be described as metaphysical. In analyzing reality, montage presupposes of its very nature the unity of meaning of the dramatic event. . . . In short, montage by its very nature rules out ambiguity of expression.[22]

Some minimalist-structuralist works can be best regarded as almost a *reductio ad absurdum* of Bazin's principles. Warhol's real-time studies of a haircut or his notorious (though rarely screened) multihour meditation upon the Empire State Building are discussed by Sitney in almost Bazinian terms: "To the catalog of the spatial strategies of the structural film must be added the temporal gift from Warhol—duration."[23] Further, and at the same time, these works reject the dynamic, pyrotechnicality of expanded cinema. Snow's forty-five-minute, fixed-camera-position zoom-in, which is the main substance of *Wavelength*, stands in contrast to *OFFON*'s cinevideo complexity.

Most minimalist-structuralist productions, in fact, constitute quintessential examples of manifest theory, theory unwritten, theory directly available in motion picture form. More, they often exhibit and clarify key concepts associated with the larger philosophical movement and related written theory analogously termed *structuralism*. One of these key concepts is the intrinsic interrelationship of those putatively separable elements of form and content.

Saussure's *Course in General Linguistics* provided foundation for most of the structuralism that (decades later) followed its posthumous publication in 1916. Recall that Saussure's lectures had envisioned a future discipline of semiotics, "a science that studies the life of signs within society."[24] While not all the cinesemiotic writings that came to almost dominate structuralist regards for film during the decade of the 1970s derived from Saussure, certainly the continental semiotics of major figures like Christian Metz and Umberto Eco did. Saussure's systemic regard for signs was at once intertransformational and synergetic, with a change in one component rarely unaffecting other components. Later semioticians explicitly enlarged Saussure's concept of sign to include not only written/spoken words but also photographic/cinematographic/videographic constructs (along with a wealth of phenomena such as sculpture and architecture). In general, such extension to symbols retained Saussure's regard for signs as relational (as opposed to substantive) entities. In this same revolutionary regard, the key relationship is that between the sign or symbol's perceived component (the tangible or empirical "signifier") and the resulting mentation (the intangible, phenomenological "signified"). For example, were the reader to behold a photograph, its perceptible tones, lines, and forms would not be the "symbol" itself (signs and symbols have no such substance in Saussure's semiotics); rather, they are only the "signifiers," the actual gestalt of the symbol being dependent upon those same consensual elements *cum* the very nontangible cognitive operations that the photograph "causes" in the reader's mentation. Thus, for Saussure, there can be no (precise) synonyms, any change on the level of signifier (what might be here termed *form*) being inextricably interrelated to the signified (rudely analogous to the quite nonstructuralist concept of *content*).

Let us consider Snow's *Wavelength* from the mutual perspective of both Saussure's and Sitney's written theory. Shot in a New York City loft over a period of several days, the film's minimal action is largely impertinent to its structuralist shape. Instead, that shape is the substance of a slow zoom (forty-five minutes long) from wide angle to telephoto. Now, typically, a cinematographic or videographic employ of a zoom-in constitutes a rather peripheral component of the work's total structure, being used—in a sense—as but one means to the simple end of recomposition. In *Wavelength*, however, this zoom becomes the dominant address; audiences are forced to attend to the particular perspective play of a slow exchange of focal lengths (in contrast to the type of perspective variation resulting from a dolly's physical move of a fixed focal-length lens through space or the abrupt exchange resulting from even more commonplace cuts: montage). Snow's directly theoretical motivation for such a minimalist restriction of cinematographic variables as that which quite aptly "shapes" *Wavelength* is an almost empirical examination. By means of such a precise reduction of variables, the work can better answer reflexivity's perennial questions regarding a given medium's intrinsic technostructural elements.[25] No amount of written theory could replace the experience of watching *Wavelength*; further, once watched, what zoom will ever be seen or employed in quite the same means-to-an-end fashion? Saussure's insistence upon the systemic bonding of signifier/signified is directly manifest in *Wavelength*'s intrinsic cinematographic concern with composition—a commutable exchange of components on the plane of signifier (here, dolly or zoom or cut) being immediately and reflexively revealed as inextricably interconnected to changes on the plane of the signified. In a directly

theoretical manner, we immediately witness the intertransformational bonding of a spurious dichotomy: form and content.

Although Sitney *explicitly* removes Robert Breer's animation from
the structural film, Sitney quickly adds, "The structural cinema has
been influenced by his achievements."[26] Breer's reflexive address is
animation's technostructural predication upon single-frame cinematography. Whereas Hans Richter's *Rhythmus 21* reflexively redefined
animation by a protodeconstructive remove from the concept of cartoon, Breer typically deconstructs the far more pervasive, insidious
connection between single-frame technostructure and animated
movement (compare the smooth movements of Richter's cubist cutouts or Oskar Fischinger's solid objects). One of Breer's directly deconstructive strategies for this reflexive reformation of animation's
ongoing escape from the confines of cartoon continuity is to use each
frame to photograph a disparate image (as opposed to slightly dis-
placed records of the same image). At twenty-four frames per second,
the psychophysiological effect is distinct from (yet similar to) superimposition; when done with color (as in Breer's 1968 work *69*), the
phenomenological, glowing, gestalt-color exists on no one frame but
is rather the projected product of groups of frames. In *Blazes* (1961),
Breer's dadaist embrace of chance has him shuffle scores of abstract
images drawn upon file cards—to which he typically gives but one
frame—with the effect of a quite manic, somewhat superimposed,
surprisingly harmonious montage. Indeed, Breer's reflexivity not only
allows us to help perfect our definition of animation but also forces
us to see that the seemingly clear distinction between montage and
animation can be readily brought to a point of ephemerality.

Almost by definition, animation embodies Sitney's structuralist
characteristic of fixed-camera position.[27] As we have seen, the rapid
montage of Fernand Léger's *Ballet Mécanique*—while likely realized
in a manner independent of a fixed camera—reflexively mimicked
animation's particular mode of movement. As early as 1929, Eisenstein
seemed to sense this similarity between rapid montage and animation
when his written theory discussed his concept of *clatter montage*.
With its Breer-like "effect almost of double exposure achieved by . . .
[the brief] length of montage pieces—two frames each," clatter montage is but one example of Eisenstein's "artificially produced image of

motion."[28] Eisenstein's best-known example of such quasi-animated motion is the rising lion in *Battleship Potemkin* (1925), which is both illustrated and discussed in *Film Form*: "Composed of three shots of three stationary marble lions at the Alupka Palace in the Crimea: a sleeping lion, an awakening lion, a rising lion. The effect is achieved by a correct calculation of the length of the second shot. Its superimposition on the first shot produces the first action. This establishes time to impress the second position on the mind. Superimposition of the third position on the second produces the second action: the lion finally rises."[29]

Independent of the contemporary accuracy of Eisenstein's decades-old psychophysiology of perception and cognition in this written theory, his classic docudrama *Battleship Potemkin* did directly scrutinize this tenuous boundary between montage and animation. A half-century later, in 1979, Gary Beydler came to produce a minimalist-structuralist work that even more directly and immediately addressed this peculiar interrelationship between montage and animation. It is interesting to note that by 1979, Sitney's prescriptions for this highly reflexive genre had reformed the short-lived coastal dichotomy addressed earlier. Beydler's *Pasadena Freeway Stills* is clearly a minimalist-structuralist West Coast work that rejects expanded cinema's technostructural complexity. Indeed, it fits Sitney's originally descriptive and eventually prescriptive definition by virtue of two structuralist characteristics: fixed-camera position and rephotography.

To describe *Pasadena Freeway Stills* is, to some extent, to mitigate its minimalist-structuralist effect for those readers who have not actually screened the film. This is not to say that any written description can in any real way replace the actual experience of the projected images. However, it is to say that the core affect of any minimalist-structuralist work depends upon each viewer—probably at different points during the work's screening—grasping Sitney's concept of shape. Such shape is nonnarrative, usually technostructurally distinct from work to work, and ultimately highly reflexive. It can, though, be rudely revealed by a description such as the one that follows—and we remain ambivalent to this particular response for that aesthetic dilemma.

Stills' minimally silent, fixed-camera projection begins and ends (some six minutes later) with the color image of a pane of glass upon which is a simple taped rectangle. A man's torso enters the frame (in real time); the man sits, and his hands begin to place and replace a series of black-and-white still photos within the 3×4 aspect ratio of the rectangle (see plate 5.2). The film begins an ever-increasing montage that removes more and more of this same, repeated action by a series of increasingly abbreviated jump cuts, until the unmoving camera is reduced to single-frame capture of each still. Somewhere, sometime during this progression, *Stills* exchanges montage for animation as audience attention is drawn toward the interior frame's black-and-white drive through tunnels on the Pasadena Freeway. The animation is highly reflexive as we witness the man's comparatively dynamic (that is, unmatched) hand positions as he holds each still in place; indeed, at one point, the film (accidentally?) slips back into montage, deconstructing the otherwise rigorously executed design. Symmetrically, *Stills* ends with increased frames (shooting on twos, threes, and so on) until we—again, somewhere/sometime—return to rapid jump cuts followed by longer takes until the final, real-time shot of the man, who stands and exits the fixed frame.

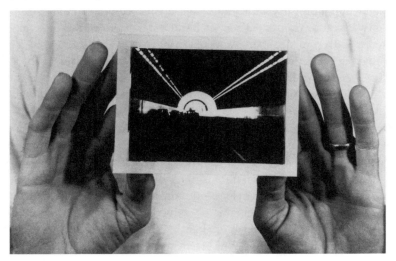

Plate 5.2. *Pasadena Freeway Stills* (1979) by Gary Beydler. Courtesy of the American Federation of Arts.

We would suspect that different audience members grasp *Pasadena Freeway Stills'* simple but complex shape at slightly different times (potentially an empirically testable conjecture). At some point, one realizes not only that the stills employed were derived from a live-action, motion-picture strip taken during a simple drive through the tunnels but also a more powerful aesthetic insight—one can anticipate and grasp the overall form of the film. That same grasp of *Stills'* unique, nonnarrative structure is to a great extent what this very experimental production is about. But it is also, if not equally, about animation, especially the interrelationships between animation and montage.[30] The subject matter of the freeway is comparatively impertinent to *Stills'* highly immediate, directly theoretical address of the same techno-structural similarities that teased both Eisenstein and Léger.

Sitney's second structural characteristic of flicker is often the product of animation as well. However, the seminal work that is most often cited to exemplify flicker films—Tony Conrad's *The Flicker* (1966)—was in the main the product of montage.[31] *The Flicker* approaches the minimalist limit, comprising alternating pure-black or pure-clear frames. As in *Pasadena Freeway Stills*, there is no sound. Further, its fleeting phenomenological artifacts are cinematographically specific, being dependent not only upon the motion picture projector's standard speed of twenty-four frames per second but upon that projector's intermittent (shutter) mechanism—a mechanism that intrinsically "flickers" (albeit at a frequency beyond the threshold of flicker fusion). There have been many flicker films made, all of which reflexively investigate this otherwise invisible phenomenon of cinematographic alterations of (lighted) image and (closed-shutter) darkness. While video analogs of flicker are quite possible, it is interesting to note that flicker films do not transfer well to video due to video's distinct method of articulating its electronic frames. Thus, one of the directly theoretical insights provided by flicker films is this provocative difference between mechanical-chemical and electronic constraints, a difference usually hidden by more typical cinematography that is designed to obscure rather than reveal the constant alternations of image and blackness.

We would like to use Joseph Anderson's also silent production of *Alpha Mandala* (1972), upon which Small collaborated, to elaborate some of the remarkable implications of this cinematographically specific technostructure. The research that preceded *Alpha Mandala* was a combination of examining extant flicker films as well as extant literature on the psychophysiological interrelationships between stroboscopic frequencies and electroencephalographic frequencies (EEG). Called *photic driving*, these interrelationships appear very precise: if subjects are confronted with a given stroboscopic frequency, their EEG readings match that frequency.[32] Reasoning that a cinematographic projector maintains a speed of twenty-four frames per second, *Alpha Mandala*'s construction was realized by animating clear "circles" on both alternate frames and on every third frame (see plate 5.3).

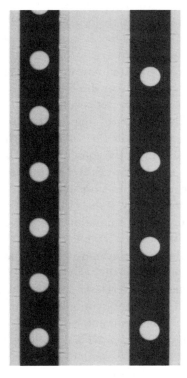

Plate 5.3. *Alpha Mandala* (1972) by Joseph Anderson and Edward Small.

The resulting intermittent photic stimulation precisely embodied the boundaries of that EEG frequency known as *alpha*. Every other frame (that is, twenty-four divided by two) provided a twelve-cycle frequency; every third frame (twenty-four divided by three) provided an eight-cycle frequency. The result was not only demonstrable (EEG) photic driving but also an elusive pattern of form and color that greatly resembled classic and contemporary mandalas.[33]

Alpha Mandala's reflexivity is directly proportional to its minimalist reduction of variables. Like most flicker films, its audience must be sophisticated enough to realize that perceived colors and patterns are derived from the minimal, binary alternation of black and white frames (a sophistication directly apprehended by a simple examination of the unprojected strip of film); greater sophistication (and greater reflexive, directly theoretical insight) is predicated upon some knowledge of the intertransformational effects produced upon this same minimal montage by the cinematographically intrinsic, otherwise almost seamless flicker of the projector's shutter. Just as there are poet's poems, flicker films are really designed for audiences of film artists or scholars who can directly grasp the work's shape and immediately appreciate its theoretical implications. For more general audiences, the photic induction of alpha rhythms is generally received as aesthetically pleasant, while the perceived, dynamic mandalas— themselves predicated upon the equally minimal, singular, circular form—often prove highly provocative, raising very pertinent questions related to the material and immaterial processes of the cinema. Likewise, *Pasadena Freeway Stills* is really designed for audiences sophisticated enough about animation's single-frame essence to be able to grasp the vast theoretical implications of its elusive exchange of montage for animation. But more general audiences can grasp the work's shape nonetheless; they can (during the film's projection) more or less anticipate the overall structure—and this general grasp is not unconnected with some seminal, fundamental insights into the nature of animation and montage. Thus, both works evidence quintessential reflexivity and provide far more sophisticated examples of direct theory than do selections from earlier genres.

Sitney's qualification that such works can "modify" his four structural characteristics will become progressively valuable as we witness the influence of minimalist-structuralist aesthetic strategies upon experimental video. Even within film, Scott MacDonald has currently come to focus upon the commonplace modification of

Sitney's fixed-camera position with single-take films.[34] Baillie's *Still Life* and Sakumi Hagiwara's *Kiri* (1971) are two examples that predate *Visionary Film*'s publication. The fact that *Kiri* ("mist") was made in Japan also demonstrates just how pervasive minimalist-structuralist strategies had become by the decade of the 1970s. *Kiri* is a fixed-camera, uncut, black-and-white record of a Japanese mountain that is (quite minimally) obscured and revealed and obscured again behind a floating, fleeting mist. The image's quality recalls *sumi-e* ink painting, and *Kiri*'s natural sound is randomly punctuated by a bell that recalls the meditative ambience of a *zendo*. More directly, the film's very absence of any montage recalls and restates, in a far more immediate fashion, the classic Eisenstein-Bazin debate that dominated written theory during the decades of the 1960s and 1970s.

Modification of Sitney's four characteristics also marks J. J. Murphy's *Print Generation* (1974). Whereas the film's loop printing is employed in a manner that could be called doctrinaire, Murphy's "rephotography" is not, strictly speaking, "off the screen." (Indeed, *Print Generation* could be considered a highly reflexive printer film, yet quite unlike the expanded cinema of O'Neill.) Again, we find ourselves in a dilemma as we write about the intricate, recursive reflexivity of this minimalist-structuralist work. Jacques Derrida's written theory on deconstruction has clearly demonstrated our society's logocentrism.[35] The very value of verbal description presupposes privilege for such left-brain processes. In clever contrast, minimalist-structuralist imperatives champion right-brain mentation: the immediate theoretical address of preemptive reflexivity. To be sure, both modes are complementary. Ideally, one should first screen such a work, and then later written/spoken explication can provide consensual cognitive elaboration and confirmation. Yet most of our readers have not screened *Print Generation*, so we would prefer to use only Murphy's own verbal description, which accompanied the film's screening at the Fifth International Forum of Young Cinema (West Berlin, 1975):

> *Print Generation* consists of sixty different images, each lasting precisely one second/twenty-four frames, which undergo a continual metamorphosis through fifty print generations—printed successively from one another—in which printing variables have

been kept as constant as possible throughout. Since contact printing alternates winds (changes focus and screen direction) in successive generations, the generations are divided accordingly into A and B winds of twenty-five generations each. The soundtrack is a direct analogue to the visuals, created by generating one minute of ocean sounds—fifty times—back and forth between two identical tape recorders, thus making an A and B track. As with the visuals, the sound was allowed to distort naturally from the process rather than through conscious or artistic manipulation. One secret of the film is this: change, measure, and relation; film as a visual experience in which mind and eye work actively in unison; an awareness of the film image as a three-layer arrangement of color emulsion—blue, green, and red—corresponding to the perceptual unfolding of those layers to the eye; a concern for a metapoetry engaging cognition and memory.

The direct aesthetic effect of *Print Generation*'s shape is far more terse, quasi-mathematical, and diagrammatic than Murphy's verbal description. Indeed, the work directly precedes the logocentrism denounced by Derrida. One can, in a sense, hold the complex shape of *Print Generation* in one's mind much as one grasps other nonlinear, simultaneous constructions such as sculpture, or driving directions within one's hometown, or the floor plan of a known building.

Recall Murphy's empirical control of variables as well as the recursive reflexivity that encompasses such details as the printer's peculiar reversal of emulsion positions and even the maximum length of the most common 16mm reel (hence Murphy's limit of fifty generations). The film itself begins with images so impoverished, so depleted of information, that some time passes before the generations of the "Hardwick Dry Cleaners," the "group of young boys," the "man sawing a log," or the "woman walking in a backyard" become clear. Again, as the images become progressively clear, the sound becomes progressively impoverished. After the film's center, the alternate image generations (that is, 2-4-6-8-10, and so on) return to greater and greater obscurity (while the sound generations cycle to greater and greater clarity).

When Sitney wrote that the "great challenge . . . of the structural film became how to orchestrate duration,"[36] his trope, "orchestrate," could prove misleading. While the entire history of experimental film/video is marked by the quest for viable structures independent from narrative, and while a great many artists (namely, Richter, Léger, Fischinger, Norman McLaren) did depend upon recourse to musical forms, such music (like narrative) is ultimately extrinsic to cinema and video both. (Sitney's implicit emphasis upon musicality is thus comparable to another, alternate, extrinsic generic recourse: painting.) Yet with minimalism-structuralism we do witness a pronounced concern for duration—with works often longer than our arbitrary half-hour characteristic of brevity. Murphy's *Print Generation* is a perfect example. But Murphy and other minimalist-structuralist artists like Beydler successfully avoid "orchestration's" tropic reliance upon music. Instead, they seek nonnarrative structures far more intrinsic to their media, structures thus powerfully open to the direct theory that follows upon their axiomatic reflexivity. *Print Generation* succeeds in structuring almost an hour of sounds and images without recourse to either narrative or music or painting. It thus caps the quest that began with *Rhythmus 21* by providing a partial but immediate answer to the complex question "What is intrinsic to cinema?" Printer generations are intrinsic. The subject matter of Murphy's sixty one-second shots is irrelevant: art has become the subject of art.

Of course, throughout this period of both expanded and minimalist-structuralist works, there are literally countless productions by such artists as Kenneth Anger (for example, *Lucifer Rising*, 1980), Bruce Baillie (for example, *Quick Billy*, 1970), Stan Brakhage (for example, *The Governor*, 1977), Bruce Conner (for example, *Valse Triste*, 1979), and Will Hindle (for example, *Chinese Firedrill*, 1968) that remain independent of these two genres.[37] Their distinctly lyric address may well retain them under our genre of underground (see figure 5.1).

Other minimalist-structuralist works like Standish Lawder's *Runaway* (1969)—a looped excerpt from an old cartoon that is subtly, electronically modulated by means of a television film chain—also vie for the subcategory of "cinevideo" since their final motion picture form resulted from rephotography off a video screen. In part, such cinevideo productions remind us that our generic characteristic of technical innovation progressively includes the pronounced research and development that came to mark then-current video technology.

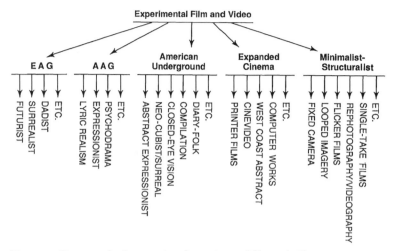

Figure 5.1. Genres and subcategories of experimental film and video.

Reconsider our term/concept *cinevideo* as emphasizing an essential commonality between mechanical-chemical and electronic constructions of moving images by implying that their (present) similarities are as interesting and as instructive as their differences. Similarity is particularly pronounced when we compare either form to theater or novels, painting or music—or any other artwork predicated upon distinct semiotic systems. But film and video's far more similar semiotic systems constitute a special bonding. While this same insight is also available from the application of systemically specific analytic tools like Herbert Zettl's "primary," "secondary," and "tertiary" motion or Metz's *grande syntagmatique*,[38] the more immediate resource of reflexivity also directly reveals that video is not just another (quicker, easier, cheaper) way of doing the same thing. Indeed, the reflexivity that we will examine in the next chapter explores not only film/video similarities but also—perhaps far more important for future decades—their often subtle differences.

6. Experimental Video

D uring the decade of the 1980s, a great many experimental films continued to be made by both established artists like Stan Brakhage and newer, younger artists who were often products of the hundreds of college and university classes devoted to film-making that had become established since the 1960s. However, the extraordinary flourish of experimental film that occurred during the 1960s and early 1970s had long since peaked. So pronounced was this reduction in quantity (and perhaps, to some extent, in quality, especially in regard to issues of innovation) that, informally, some film scholars were wont to suggest that the entire experimental endeavor was either moribund or already dead. One of this chapter's tasks is to argue against that suggestion. While our argument is not a complex one, we are puzzled as to why the plethora of experimental video productions that we will draw upon to support it remains overlooked by those academic historians, critics, and theorists who have devoted themselves to experimental film. Recall that one of the eight characteristics of this major genre has been a particular affinity for technological innovation. Gene Youngblood's concept of expanded cinema was greatly predicated upon this affinity's eventual embrace of electronic devices, both video and computer systems (which were typically interconnected with cathode ray tube displays). To be sure, much minimalist-structuralist production began as a sort of counterbalance to expanded cinema's ever-increasing technological complexity. However, video's multiannual gains in reliability, ease of operation, and quite stunning economic advantage resulted in the ongoing confluence of cinematic and television technologies. Just as cinema's nitrate stock yielded (with some loss, some gain) to acetate stocks, just as broadcast television evolved (and to some extent devolved) with the inventions of videotape recorders and later videocassettes, so did film's mechanical-chemical qualities become augmented by video's far more electronic resources. But we must realize that this was indeed more a matter of augmentation than replacement, and the term *confluence* embodies an image of merger in which each contributive tributary melds into a larger body. We personally predict that the future will see neither film nor video nor the mere sum of the contribution of each but rather a distinct product, the gains of which will likely overshadow the losses.

Our concept of *technostructure* contends that such changes and exchanges of technology and techniques are inseparable from structural changes and are thereby extraordinarily consequential. Here we would point to paradox in our employ of the descriptor *extraordinarily*. If structure is the interrelationship of the parts to the whole, how can one consider any constitutive part as extraordinary? In this case, we would argue that technological contribution is often so subtle, and extant theoretical frameworks are often so rudimentary, that few scholars of film and video still seem unable to appreciate the intricate interplay embodied by the concept of technostructure.

Again, our major exception is film historian Raymond Fielding. Allow us to iterate Fielding's introduction to *A Technological History of Motion Pictures and Television*, which clearly frames the evolving interrelationship between technical and structural change:

> There is a temptation for film historians in particular to interpret the development of the motion picture teleologically, as if each generation of workers had sketched out the future of the art far in advance of the technology required for its realization. In fact, however, the artistic evolution of the film has always been intimately associated with technological change, just as it has, in less noticeable fashion, in the older arts. Just as the painter's art has changed with the introduction of different media and processes, just as the forms of symphonic music have developed with the appearance of new kinds of instruments, so has the elaboration and refinement of film style followed from the introduction of more sophisticated machinery. The contribution of a Porter, Ince, or Griffith followed as much from the availability of portable cameras and improved emulsions as it

did from their individual vision and talent. Similarly, the cinema verité movement of today could not possibly have appeared and prospered . . . prior to the miniaturization of camera and sound equipment, and with dramatic improvements in film stocks. If the artistic and historical development of film and television are to be understood, then so must the peculiar marriage of art and technology which prevails in their operations.[1]

Fielding's "intimate association" could suggest causality; our own structuralist premises prefer an intertransformative regard. Thus, while this concept of technostructure is greatly indebted to Fielding's innovative research, he may not agree that concomitance of technological change and structural change maps a more accurate relationship. Still, building upon the theoretical contributions of scholars like Fielding, we would suggest that the same technological impetus for imagery that photography exhibited was technologically transformed first into cinema's (eventual) amalgam of sound and image and then into video's more purely electronic constructions. And although, in structure, the relationship among elements is far more significant than any element itself, in structure the greater does control the lesser, and Fielding's insights help reveal just how great that technologic contribution can be.

The evolution of cathode ray tube (CRT) technology is within the lived experience of most current scholars of film and video. The 1950s was the decade of live broadcast television; structures transformed with the 1960s development of videotape recorders and transformed again by the portable video equipment that resulted from the 1970s introduction of videocassettes. The 1980s was dominated by the wedding of microcomputers with CRT displays, evident in such modes as interactive videogames and in such fields as computer animation. Throughout, far more research and development took place in the realm of electronic constructions of moving images than in the realm of mechanical-chemical constructions. In part, this research has been economically driven (for example, one could copy literally hours of color/sound video for a few dollars; in contrast, cinema's complex laboratory procedures coupled with the high cost of silver would drive a 16mm color/sound copy to several hundred dollars—perhaps several thousand, depending upon length).

It is therefore not surprising that experimental artists who worked outside the combined support and restrictions of industry economics would be attracted to video's versatility and economy as they continued the quest—which we saw begin in Europe in the 1920s—for structures beyond commonplace narrative. Further, as we have witnessed to some extent already, the scope of this quest was hardly confined to the United States. In fact, Malcolm Le Grice's *Abstract Film and Beyond* surveys contemporary experimental production in Europe, where our major genre originated and only temporarily halted, yielding to North American developments. Le Grice is consonant with our thesis when he writes that the impetus for experimental film production on both continents was "to develop the medium as an area within which 'film thought' can take place, rather than as a tool for the expression of literary ideas."

In film, as in art [for example, painting], the organization of the elements, qualities and characteristics of the medium is a means of intelligent thought, in its own right, and we should not be surprised if the patterns of thought which we encounter via this mode are different in kind to those which derive from other media. In many ways our minds and eyes are not culturally attuned to the conditions of thinking directly through film, so we feel the need to translate that experience into a more familiar mode. Not only is the "art" of film itself little developed in plastic terms but the critical language to deal with it is even less so. Most of the major critics of cinema have a strong literary bias, being more at home with narrative, dramatic, symbolist or surrealist forms.[2]

Le Grice also agrees with our own survey that this impetus to transcend literary forms began with a comparable dependence upon equally extrinsic, though appreciably nonnarrative, media. Early experimental films sought "inspiration in the state of [then] contemporary non-figurative painting. Whilst their notions of time-structure were mostly drawn from music, their visual aspects were directly relatable to the painting of the period."[3] However, later experimental films—as we have seen, especially in the genre of minimalism-structuralism—have, through progressive reflexivity, extended into what

Le Grice calls an "essentially cinematic" state: "Film has moved progressively towards a form, which is not dependent on other areas of
art for the source of its conventions, not only breaking the strangle-
hold of theatre and literature, but also developing past the alternative
dependence on painting and music. Since the war [World War II] we
have seen the gradual emergence of a film art, which is genuinely cinematographic in concept."[4] Perhaps because of Le Grice's devotion to
the "genuinely cinematographic," his early, highly theoretical studies
seem to ignore experimental video. Aptly, one of the few early studies
on experimental video—Jonathan Price's *Video-Visions: A Medium
Discovers Itself*—was published the same year (1977) as Le Grice's
and explicitly addresses an analogous quest for what might well be
called the "genuinely videographic." Writing that video artists strive to
address that which is unique to video, Price explains: "Not imitation
film, but genuine video, not theatrical photographs, but live video. The
current American ideal, it seems, is to create an intensely personal
style as one explores the unique capabilities of video, consciously
comparing it with [other] media such as painting, words, or music."[5]

This chapter's historical survey of experimental video will present
two complementary directions. Many experimental videos underscore the concept of cinevideo in which the similarities between mechanical-chemical and electronic constructions can be clearly more a
matter of degree than of kind (as in either's comparison to literature,
drama, painting, or music). On the other hand, a great many experimental video works do seek, quite reflexively, to reveal the subtle
differences between film and video—and such productions, in the long
run, may well prove to be the most valuable, exhibiting theory's pre-
dictive power for hints as to what this ongoing confluence will yield.

If the concept of technostructure is accurate, it can be coupled
with Ferdinand de Saussure's profound insight regarding the inextricable, intertransformative bonding of any sign/symbol's signifier
and signified. Technological changes are thus consequential. While
film and video symbols may be similar, they can never be the same.
Experimental video directly, immediately examines some of these
ultimately myriad differences. Nearly half a century ago, the written
theory of Marshall McLuhan addressed at least one such difference,
albeit hyperbolically: "The mode of the TV image has nothing in

common with film or photo. . . . The TV image is not a *still* shot. It is not a photo in any sense, but a ceaselessly forming contour of things limned by the scanning-finger. The resulting plastic contour appears by light *through*, not light *on*, and the image so formed has the quality of sculpture and icon, rather than of picture."[6] All video, experimental and otherwise, retains this potential for an aesthetic far closer to that of stained glass or neon lighting than to the reflected light of motion picture projection. And such "mere" technological exchange on the level of signifier will always remain, covertly or overtly, on the level of signified as well.

Still, this chapter contends that the productions it presents are part of a decades-old major genre: experimental motion pictures. Again, recall our eight generic characteristics of acollaborative construction, economic independence, brevity, an affinity for ongoing technological innovation, the phenomenology of mental imagery, an avoidance of verbal language, nonnarrative strategies, and a pronounced reflexivity. To be sure, all characterize experimental video as well as (if not better than) they have characterized experimental film. For example, whereas sound is both costly and complicated in film, it is costless and easy in video; yet a great many of the video productions that we will survey either deemphasize sound by employing only subtle, natural, real-time recordings, or in some cases, these works avoid sound altogether, choosing instead Brakhage's aesthetic of silence. Both sound modes, incidentally, make the video works highly international in that their resulting insistence upon nonverbal visual structures transcends at least geolinguistic (if not first-world culture) barriers.

Our selections are in fact international. For the most part, the U.S. productions examined are from a New York City video archive: Electronic Arts Intermix. Canadian productions are from either Le Videographe or PRIM Media Arts Centre, two archives in the predominantly French-speaking city of Montreal, Canada.[7] They cover a period from 1973 through 1991, with the majority of titles following the early-1970s introduction of half-inch videocassettes. It is important to emphasize these dates since they encompass the publication of P. Adams Sitney's *Visionary Film* and the cinematic success of our last chapter's genre of minimalism-structuralism. In fact, as we argue that experimental film and experimental video are not separate movements but rather diachronic stages of one long, never fully inter-rupted movement that can best be regarded as experimental motion pictures, we are struck by the pronounced link provided by mini-malist-structuralist aesthetics. Allow us to review that aesthetic with some insights and elaborations by Le Grice.

In *Abstract Film and Beyond*, Le Grice pays a somewhat reluctant homage to Sitney's term and concept *structuralism*. On the one hand, while Le Grice sees no "simple, obvious connection" between Sitney's concept and the larger, philosophical position, he does concede that "it is possible to find some parallels."[8] On the other hand, while Le Grice strives to reform what he calls Sitney's "loose concept of shape," he agrees that this concept does reveal "definable characteristics or regions of cinematic inquiry."[9] Ultimately, however, writing five years later and a continent away, Le Grice sought to reform and extend Sitney's original position:

> In tracing the development of this new formal tendency, I shall accept the broad divergence of the experimentation, and in-stead of seeing those factors which Sitney refers to, like flicker effect, loop printing, and re-photography, as identifying char-acteristics of a category, I shall see them as concerns or di-rections of inquiry in a broad, formal tendency. I shall add to them a number of other concerns, like celluloid as material, the projection as event, duration as a concrete dimension. I shall also modify Sitney's characteristic of the fixed camera in favor of a more general exploration of camera-functioning and the consequences of camera-motion or procedure in their various forms. I shall refer generally to the question of procedure as a determinant of form.[10]

Le Grice's "question of procedure as a determinant of form" aptly bonds many of the experimental films he discusses with the experi-mental video productions we will examine in this chapter. For exam-ple, the three segments that make up Peter Campus's *Three Transi-tions* (1973) are highly reflexive video studies that are all quite specific to video, the first of which depends upon two fixed cameras to provide an insightful exploration of Le Grice's camera functioning. Again, no verbal description can capture the directly theoretical address of Campus's all but silent investigation of two uncut, superimposed video shots of him slicing and tearing a hole through a paper barrier and crawling through that hole. Verbal language's abstraction and linearity stand antithetical to Campus's concrete, simultaneous display of information. The best hope may be a diagrammatic resource: a bird's-eye view/schematic (see figure 6.1).

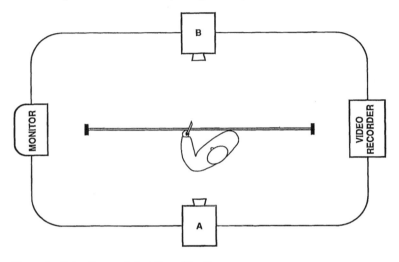

Figure 6.1. Peter Campus's first "transition."

When the brief "transition" begins, Campus is seen from camera A, standing before a brownish wall. He proceeds to cut through the wall (which we then realize is a paper backdrop), and, while listening to the cutting occur, we are struck by a superimposed knife blade that seems to exit Campus's back. As he enlarges the hole and crawls through, we realize that a second camera (B) was running throughout. The work ends with Campus taping up the hole and exiting the (second) fixed frame, returning us to video's illusion of depth, which directly collapsed during the earlier superimpositions.

The work is clearly within the reflexive aesthetic of minimalism-structuralism and really remains beyond the bounds of film (the electronic superimposition is far easier than superimposition using film; also, Campus constantly checks an offscreen monitor for his various actions—film precludes such instant interaction with the image). Likewise, Campus's other two "Transitions" from 1973, the year before *Visionary Film* was published, are quite video-specific in their reflexivity. One is a single-take close-up of Campus's head as he applies a chroma-key-colored cream to his face while employing a videotaped similar image (initially hidden) as a sort of electronic mirror (which the chroma-key matte progressively uncovers as the cream is applied). Campus uses the monitor to keep both heads lined up. Finally, the last transition is a close-up of Campus's face on a piece of paper (again electronically keyed to a videotape input): as he burns the paper, his taped face disappears. All three segments are highly reflexive and quite theoretical in their direct, immediate address of elements specific to video's otherwise bonded similarities with film. While the date of *Three Transitions* follows the availability of half-inch videocassettes, it demanded industry and studio resources that could provide then very expensive chroma-key technology. The segments are otherwise independent.

Campus's 1974 *R-G-B* ("red-green-blue") is not predicated upon studio resources and, in fact, could find analog in cinema—with subtle differences. *R-G-B* also depends upon the fixed-camera, single-take procedure that characterizes so many minimalist-structuralist works. Campus himself sits before a video camera (with an automatic aperture) and progressively places and removes a red filter, then a green filter, and then a blue filter over the lens; the natural sound records the brief aperture compensation for each gelatin sheet's filter factor. He ends the work by adding the filters until the cumulative colors bring the screen to black. As with *Three Transitions*, the work is acollaborative, economically independent, brief (both works run about five minutes each, although videotape is inexpensive and makes cost no concern here), nonnarrative, and so nonverbal that written descriptions become a study in inadequacy. Both *Three Transitions* and *R-G-B* are clearly reflexive electronic extensions of the minimalist-structuralist films we examined in the last chapter.

Like those of Peter Campus, Stephen Beck's U.S. productions are distributed by New York's Electronic Arts Intermix (EAI). Beck's nine-minute *Video Weavings* (1977) follows upon the availability of both half-inch videocassette technology and progressive availability of personal analog computers. In many ways, *Video Weavings* is an extension of Youngblood's expanded cinema, though in purely electronic rather than cinematographic form. More precisely, *Video Weavings* follows the abstraction we have seen in Hans Richter's *Rhythmus 21*, Oskar Fischinger's *Composition in Blue*, Norman Mc-Laren's *Begone Dull Care*, and Jordan Belson's *Allures*. (Beck has in fact collaborated with Belson on at least one project.)[11] However, Beck's CRT canvas is marked by McLuhan's insight of nonphotographic light plus the very signature of computer/CRT pixels, which, by creating abstract images often mandalic in structure, are devoted to patterns that recall Native American rugs and tapestries (see plate 6.1). Again, the core characteristics of acollaborative auteurism, economic independence, brevity, an affinity for technological innovation (Beck constructed his own video synthesizers with computer controls), mandalic mental imagery, avoidance of verbal language (*Weavings*' sound is a simple musical score), nonnarrative structures, and video-specific reflexivity (*Weavings*, again, embodies McLuhan's stained-glass aesthetic) are all readily applicable. Beck's own writings on his videographics underscore many of these characteristics: "Personally I have been interested in the symbolic, ideographic, and nonobjective modes of images, those which originate internally within the mind's eye. Affected by images of color and movement, I was led to invent the Direct Video Synthesizer instrument. Conceiving of it as a compositional instrument rather than a distortion device, I incorporated a theory of visual 'ingredients' of color, form, motion, and texture into electronic circuit modules which generate these building-block elements on a television display. The images that appear are due to the interplay of electronic vibrations, established by the artist, [who] creates them."[12]

Artists such as Beck and Campus are recognized pioneers in experimental video. They follow upon the groundbreaking work of Korean-born Nam June Paik, who, from John Hanhardt's perspective, began the "transformation of [broadcast] television into a post-modern art form."[13] Paik's video constructions were often predicated upon a neo-dadaist aesthetic that also can inform the three major modes of experimental video's exhibition: broadcast TV, gallery installations, and videotape rentals (the latter perhaps being the closer analog to experimental film). Hanhardt writes of a 1963 gallery exhibition:

Plate 6.1. *Video Weavings* (1977) by Stephen Beck. Photo courtesy of Electronic Arts Intermix.

Certainly the key figure in the history of video art is Nam June Paik, who was given a comprehensive retrospective exhibition in 1982 at the Whitney Museum of American Art and whose work has explored all areas and forms of video. In 1963, in an exhibition entitled "Exposition of Music-Electronic Television," at the Galerie Parnasse, Paik included prepared televisions—sets whose components had been altered to produce unexpected effects—as part of his performance and installation. It was the first time Paik appropriated television technology and it signaled the beginning of a lifelong effort to deconstruct and demystify television. With sets randomly distributed in all positions throughout the gallery, each television became an instrument, removed from its customary context, handled and manipulated in a direct and physical way. The exteriors were marked up and cluttered with bottles and other objects, while chairs were scattered about the space. The scanning mechanism in the television was also manipulated, affecting the reception of broadcast images. Paik's prepared televisions were his first video sculptures.[14]

Further, Hanhardt's pioneers like Paik and Campus typically did not come to experimental video from experimental film (of course, there are exceptions, such as Ed Emshwiller); rather, they came from "other fields such as music, performance, dance, and sculpture."[15] Indeed, Hanhardt's essay emphasizes not the (characteristic) similarities between experimental film and video but rather the video-quest for that which is intrinsic to its forms and functions, in spite of its eclectic appropriations: "By extension, video art is ontologically different from film and the other visual arts[,] yet, as I noted, it does not exist in a vacuum unaffected by the aesthetic concerns of painting, sculpture, performance art, film, music, theater, and dance. It appropriates aspects of these forms and transforms them into a richly suggestive and complex iconography of genres and styles. At present, the discourse called video art confronts the text of the art object, which is codified strictly by a market created by other definitions and art forms. Video is on the 'cutting edge' of expression, as new technologies open up possibilities for image making."[16] Many such experimental video constructions thus began to go beyond minimalist-structuralist links to experimental film as part of this highly reflexive quest for video essence. Still, we contend that their relationship to those films is fundamental.

Barbara Buckner's silent *Hearts* (1979) exhibits such a video-specific and purely right-brain beauty that one fears giving it too much verbal description. The work's main motif is a series of simple, often mandalic heart shapes—drawn or cut out as mattes—interspersed with quiet, nonnarrative associations (for example, Breer-like abstractions; a silhouetted, highly electronic tree; and so on). At times, superimposures are subtly and fleetingly added; at times, a given heart becomes a rude matte, a frame for sometimes symbolic, alternating abstract and representational, static or dynamic interior images (see plate 6.2). Buckner's reflexivity remains video-specific, and *Hearts* often depends upon commonplace video artifacts for its quasi-metamorphic alterations of image: video roll, mistracking, exchanges of aperture, extremes of contrast, reduction of color to monochrome, and a defocused video camera. One sits amazed at the extraordinary range of permutations available from technical resources, which anyone who has had to adjust a television set, videocassette recorder, or video camera will directly grasp. And what is "grasped" is always contradistinct to cinema. Both Buckner's *Hearts* and *Heads* (1980) reveal an intrinsically beautiful, intrinsically video reflexivity, which, following Brakhage, cleaves to an aesthetic of silence to insist upon the dominance of the (mental) image.[17]

Plate 6.2. *Hearts* (1979) by Barbara Buckner. Photo courtesy of Electronic Arts Intermix.

Bill Viola's video work constitutes a pronounced contrast to Buckner's. On the one hand, his natural-sound accompanied images lack Buckner's highly transformational aesthetic of electronic collages. On the other hand, at least some of Viola's production is clearly influenced by minimalism-structuralism. About twenty minutes long, Viola's *Ancient of Days* (1979–81), for example, comprises five fixed-camera vignettes, all of which exemplify Le Grice's extension to "a more general exploration of [video] camera-functioning and the consequences of camera-motion or procedures in their various forms." In the first vignette, a table and chair rise, phoenix-like, from their ashes as a videotape is rerecorded in reverse; the second is a day-long, elusively dissolved study of the Washington Monument under transient, natural light (changing markedly with clear skies, morning shadows, afternoon clouds, and oncoming dusk). The third vignette depends upon a fixed though moving camera that extends from a city roof (or window) on a shaft, upon a kind of right-angle "tripod" that allows the camera to rotate precisely 180 degrees from an inverted (dawn) view of the street below to a dusk view of the same street's opposite direction; throughout, elusive dissolves of both natural image and natural sound can trick the eye into seeing a series of separate streets rather than a fixed position modified by a unique tilt along with natural changes of daylight. The fourth vignette depends upon two fixed cameras: the first at the base of Mount Fuji, the second at a busy shopping center of a large Japanese city. The two positions are linked by a video recording of the first setting being played upon a giant TV screen in the shopping center of the second setting.

The final vignette of Viola's *Ancient of Days* pays homage to countless still-life paintings. Before the fixed video camera is a simple set: a table upon which is a ticking clock and a vase of flowers plus what appears to be a simple landscape painting upon the wall. At first, only the clock's pendulum appears to provide us any movement (indeed, the clock's real-time ticking can dominate the static image). Then one begins to see that the painting is a rather cleverly disguised monitor that is playing back a videotape of a landscape changing in the minimalist-structuralist fashion of Sakumi Hagiwara's *Kiri*. As we will see later in this chapter, Viola's production extends beyond the bounds of minimalism-structuralism, but *Ancient of Days* is exemplary in its ability to reveal clear links with the experimental film of earlier chapters (not only because of these minimalist-structuralist elements but again because *Days* can be readily characterized by a collaborative construction, economic independence, brevity, avoidance of verbal language, nonnarrative structures, and a reflexivity often specific to the new electronic technology of video).

These same links with minimalism-structuralism plus our generic characteristics apply equally well to a great number of experimental video productions from Montreal. Especially interesting is Productions Réalisations Indépendantes de Montréal (PRIM), which maintains and distributes over two hundred videos, most of which are experimental by virtue of our eight characteristics. Further, many PRIM productions evidence an aesthetic drawn from minimalism-structuralism. For example, Richard Barbeau's *Roulement de Billes* (1985) is a nine-minute, largely fixed-camera study of various-sized ball bearings a woman rolls upon various-sized framed glass plates. The adjective *various* can only hint at the sometimes subtle, sometimes abrupt exchanges of glass or bearings resulting from Barbeau's clever cuts. Without recourse to dissolve and depending upon the woman's relatively minimal movements, ball bearings become larger, then smaller, and then still larger, each creating its own sound upon the fragile glass surface. We are always aware of the glass and are at once relieved and surprised when, at times, it does shatter; we are also progressively aware of the sound. Indeed much of *Rolling Balls'* reflexivity is in Barbeau's play of video's direct sound against occasional counterpoint (for example, hockey crowds cheering). The work is quite independent, acollaborative, nonnarrative, and so nonverbal that it is assured of an international audience.

A bit more collaborative, though equally nonverbal, is Neam Cathod's *Antiqua 78 R.P.M.* (1985), a ten-minute cinevideo production based upon video transfers and transformation of super-8mm footage of an old cathedral. These images (somewhat structurally) are looped and slowly staccato-step-projected in counterpoint to an old, scratched recording of church choir music. "Neam Cathod" is the artistic credit for PRIM's director, Jean Decarie, whose musical specialization marks *Antiqua*'s sound, which also begins to loop, then slow down, and then transform in an elaborate synthetic mix. Without recourse to story or words, *Antiqua* provides more of a religio-political commentary than the pure reflexivity we have examined throughout this book. But then, as we have seen, cinevideo embodies its own particular theoretical address.

This powerful mixture of ideology and reflexivity characterizes the two works—both from Electronic Arts Intermix—that chronologically cap our video survey. The first is a 1990 production from Brazilian videomaker Eder Santos, the less than eight-minutes-long *Não Vou á Àfrica Porque Tenho Plantão* (*I Cannot Go to Africa Because I Am on Duty*). EAI's catalog description frames and interprets this international cinevideo mixture of super-8mm film and deconstructive video records and processes:

In this vivid pastiche of images, music and text, Santos addresses technology and image-making in the context of cultural formation. Writes Santos: "Technology is explored in terms of information speed—a feature that makes popular absorption and understanding all the harder. Metaphorically, this process is akin to obtaining information through the ultra-condensation of mere legends and subtitles. Though this may occur in developed countries, such a process displays and unleashes its greatest vigor in a culture such as Brazil's. *I Cannot Go to Africa Because I Am on Duty* indirectly touches upon values: instead of being concerned with the information-absorption process and with the likelihood of controlling the image-producing process, we are hellbent on running a race, whose sole goal is to employ the latest technological innovation in terms of image production."[18]

Finally, Rea Tajiri's highly reflexive *History and Memory* (1991) constitutes a complex transgeneric blend of fictive, documentary, and experimental characteristics. Half an hour long and more collaborative than the other videos we have examined, *History and Memory* also has some elements of both the diary-folk and compilation work discussed earlier. But Tajiri's aesthetic is much closer to what Fredric Jameson terms "that pure and random play of signifiers that we call postmodernism."[19] The following description is from EAI:

Focusing on the internment of Japanese-Americans during World War II, this powerful and poignant work examines the rewriting of history through media representation. In a pastiche of film images, written text, voiceover and video, Tajiri interweaves collective history and personal memory. The attack on Pearl Harbor is seen through anonymous archival footage, Hollywood's *From Here to Eternity*, a filmed re-staging and a news report. The Japanese-American internment is similarly reconstructed. "Who chose what story to tell?" asks Tajiri. Referring to things that happened in the world with cameras watching, things that we re-stage to have images of them, and things that are observed only by the spirits of the dead, Tajiri reclaims history and memory by inserting her own video footage and narrative voice, and her mother's recollections of her family's internment.[20]

The progressive availability of VHS and progressively less expensive, more compact video provided extraordinary promise for the kind of experimental production distributed by archives like PRIM and EAI. This experimental turn to video's electronic resources should be no more unexpected or unexplained than this major genre's 1920s turn to animation, its 1930s turn to 16mm and sound, and its later employ of color, step printers, and so on. Indeed, experimental film/video's affinity for new technologies in the year that the first edition of *Direct Theory* was published seemed to be a perpetual characteristic that would likely incorporate upcoming HDTV (high-definition television), LCD (liquid crystal displays), and interactive compact disc digital devices. As we rewrite this text, it is hard to recall the "predigital world."

This chapter's survey is also highly selective. Countless video artists are overlooked. From EAI alone, names like Kit Fitzgerald and John Sanborn come to mind. Montreal's Le Videographe and PRIM serve scores of Canadian artists. And these archives themselves constitute only a small part of an international body of work.

However, we would like to end this chapter with a return to the work of one American video artist whose best-known productions deconstruct the very concept of major genre. Bill Viola's productions often seem to rush beyond the reach of scholarly categories. Works like *Hatsu Yume* and *Chott el-Djerid* are perhaps "pangeneric," transcending the actuality and experimental major genres whose composite aegis they both claim and exceed.

Viola has been a particularly successful video artist. His 1979 *Chott el-Djerid* (*A Portrait in Light and Heat*) won Grand Prize at the Portopia International Video Art Festival held in Kobe, Japan, in 1981. He was in Japan during 1980 and 1981. There, at Sony's Atsugi Plant, he completed *Hatsu Yume* (*First Dream*). He currently works out of Los Angeles, California.

Viola has completed a great many other video works, now distributed by such organizations as EAI. His central concerns—in both his fine writings and major video productions—are the very aesthetic issues of perception and related cognitive modes like memory. We note that the Greek etymology of *aesthetics* indicates a protoempirical regard for matters of sensation and perception. We have not totally lost this sense of aesthetic, as is clear in such modern terms as *anesthetic* (literally, no sensation/perception) and *synaesthetic* (discussed earlier as sensory crossover). Still, to employ *aesthetic* with that meaning today is quite revisionist. Since Alexander Gottlieb Baumgarten's *Aesthetica* (1750), the term has instead come to designate prescriptive issues of taste in the arts, as well as general considerations of the nature of beauty.

Nonetheless, to speak of aesthetics in regard to Viola, one has to embrace that same revisionist and ancient sense (literally) of the term. *Chott el-Djerid*, for example, is a minimalist, half-hour study of Sahara mirages, the real subject of which is human perception (or, reflexively, the differences and similarities between video records and our phenomenology of perception). The work's subtle, direct sound makes it seem almost silent as the nonnarrative, slow montage excludes left-brain affinities for words and numbers. The videography is exquisite and the resulting mood and emotion really too ineffable for critical capture. Likewise, *Hatsu Yume* is difficult to describe properly. As signaled by its title, the work's address has the quality of a remembered dream. In spite of Sony's support, all videography, sound (subtle, direct, almost wordless), and editing (including temporally ambiguous slow motion) are from Viola's hand, Viola's eye. The colors are incomparable captures or constructions, quietly bespeaking the artist's perfect grasp of his equipment. Throughout we are a disembodied eye and a progressively sensitive ear enjoying a dreamlike, non-narrative tour of Japan's resorts, markets, cities, and lush bamboo groves—the texture so rich one synaesthetically feels the very fabric of Viola's (ultimately) electronic leaves and stalks.

Early in *Hatsu Yume*, Viola presents us with a fixed-camera image of a rugged rock—perhaps a boulder, perhaps a mountain; we are not sure. Since we have no reference for scale while we follow the minimalist play of light and shadow upon this subject's brown surface, Viola reflexively comments upon the play of perspective inherent in any film or video lens. Only when people begin to appear (slowly and in slowed, staccato, video-reconstructed motion) do we gain an at times equally deceptive sense of this form's scale. The first people, far behind it, directly collapse the possible mountain-sized object to what is now more likely a gigantic boulder. Later, closer people again allow audience redefinition of scale until, near the end of this long, fixed-frame segment, a man walks directly adjacent to what we can finally establish as a really small rock, about a foot high. Thus Viola teases us into a highly theoretical guessing game; thus Viola teaches us about the bionic differences between eyes and lenses, which Rudolf Arnheim addressed a half-century earlier in his written theory.

It is strange to relate Arnheim with Viola. *Hatsu Yume*, for example, is recalled as largely realist or representational rather than transformative. So "straight" is Viola's video recording that one would readily liken *Hatsu Yume* to Ralph Steiner's H_2O. Indeed, one could argue that in spite of *Hatsu Yume*'s title and the work's acollaborative independence and lack of narrative or narration (or any words not Japanese), what we have here is a somewhat documentary portrait of Japan's face—urban and rural, daytime and nighttime. Indeed, one would seem to be better served by Siegfried Kracauer's concept of "a marked affinity for the visible world around us" than by any appeal to Arnheim's transformational written theory, and perhaps by any real relation to experimental categorization. But then one recalls *Hatsu Yume*'s quiet reflexivity as well as dazzling sections, such as the play of neon lights upon a rain-soaked windshield and natural prisms of wiper and water streaks that challenge the best computer graphics. Is this work not exemplarily experimental? Thus, Viola's constructions deconstruct and defy many of the categories that inform this entire book. *Hatsu Yume* quietly, lyrically reforms written theory and directly reveals just how arbitrary are our articulations, our boundaries, and our categories by which we seek to comprehend but which can equally turn traitor to blind us to both art and vision's far more infinite possibilities.

In an article on video as art published in a 1984 issue of the *Journal of Film and Video*, Viola came to quote the Persian sage Rumi on perception in a fashion that recalls the painter Paul Klee's more contemporary and more Western contention that art does not reproduce what we see but rather makes us see: "New organs of perception come into being as a result of necessity. Therefore, we should increase our necessity so that we may increase our perception."[21] We believe that, for Viola, classic video was basically a device that could increase our sensory "necessity" in just such a precisely aesthetic manner. Such sensory increase has always been art's primary purpose, hence the original, diachronic meaning of the term *aesthetic* as a *scientia cognitionis sensitivae* ("science of sensory cognition"), strikingly similar to the concept of direct theory, which is the theme of this book.

We have covered eight decades in the development of our major genre. However, what prescience is available suggests revolutionary technological changes that better serve the same impetus that governed the fine artists of the European avant-garde, the independent filmmakers of the American avant-garde and underground, and the expanded and minimalist-structuralist work that began to yield to new forms. These changes are as inevitable as they will prove consequential, because there can be no change of technologies independent of structural changes. Just as form/content can retain only its essential bond, there can be no exchange of tools without a perhaps concomitant, perhaps causal exchange of structure. For structure is ultimately the vast, ineffable interrelationship of all the parts to the whole; in structure all real change in systemic, technostructural exchanges will always prove one of the covertly commutable components of any aesthetic enterprise: thus the digital revolution.

The American semiotician Charles Sanders Peirce contended that the philosophic discipline of logic is really a semiotic science of the "general laws of signs." Like his (apparently unknown to him) Swiss contemporary Saussure, Peirce also recognized a distinction between arbitrary signs (such as words or numbers) and those more motivated entities (such as pictures), which he called icons. If verbal *discursus* is subject to the laws of *logos*, can we not conclude that Peirce's iconic discourse is comparably subject? For clarity, we would provisionally term such iconic semiotic ordinance *pictos*. Further, experimental motion pictures' major function has always been a truly theoretical attempt to explore and establish the *pictos* of our civilization's most complex and contemporary modes of pictures, cinematographic and electronic constructs, through an iterative resource generally termed *reflexivity*.

Robert Stam's *Reflexivity in Film and Literature*, while well removed from the concept of direct theory, does confirm some of the key premises of our own thesis. Quoting Christian Metz on the "specifically cinematic dimension of reflexivity," Stam asks the perennial question for the entire history of experimental film and video: "Apart from the broader narrative and rhetorical strategies available to both novel and film, how can the cinema illuminate its specific textual processes?"[22] Although Stam "does not generally emphasize the avant-garde,"[23] his occasional address of works by artists such as Bruce Conner and Michael Snow clearly confirms their rich reflexivity. To be sure, Stam's own thesis is designed to present reflexivity's broadest scope: "The penchant for reflexivity must be seen as symptomatic of the methodological self-scrutiny typical of contemporary thought, its tendency to examine its own terms and procedures. Thus we find reflexivity forming parts of diverse fields and universes of discourse."[24]

Experimental motion pictures can be better, if not best, understood as one such "universe of discourse." Distinct from, yet coordinate to, the alternate major genres of fictive narratives and nonfiction documentaries, its function is neither to entertain nor to persuade but rather to examine the quite omnipresent yet still little understood *pictos* that marks and measures our postmodern milieu. While it alone will never fully schematize this rapidly expanding semiotic subject, experimental motion pictures' contribution is exceptionally, singularly heuristic. This contribution, we have argued, constitutes the closest answer to that "complicated problem" that Metz identified as "the equivalence of the metalanguage. . . . An exposé written about the cinema is not of the same form as what it is talking about, contrary to what occurs in the theory of literature. Inversely, the utilization of the cinema as a metalanguage reflected by (and reflecting upon) itself is still an uncommon and very difficult operation, for it is not rooted in the rich reflective past which exists for written works."[25]

Metz's adjudication of this "average degree of theoretical maturity" in cinema was published decades ago. Often overlooked, experimental work—both before and after Metz's 1974 publication of *Language and Cinema*—can vastly increase Metz's degree in direct proportion to this major genre's really quite common reflexivity. We have chosen to identify and conceptualize that particular increase as direct theory. Finally, as we begin our final chapter, we move into the most current technostructural cutting edge: the "digital revolution."

7. Digital Experimental Motion Pictures

What might the digital age hold for the major genre of avant-garde/experimental productions? We believe that this particular technological change will prove so vast and so long-lasting that, at best, our futurism is but "seeing through a glass, darkly." Indeed, our very expectations are predicated upon our distinct blend of Ferdinand de Saussure's semiotic heritage and the technostructural historiography of film scholar Raymond Fielding.

However, we are hardly the only theorists bent upon this quest. Decades ago, Marshall McLuhan gave us all a theoretician's heads-up when he insisted that the difference between the mechanical-chemical system of motion pictures and the electronic system of television was not merely a difference of degree. After McLuhan's death in 1980, the charged coupled device replaced cathode ray tubes in portable television systems, which had been introduced some twenty years earlier with Sony's reel-to-reel Portapack system. The result of this change was the advent of what we call video. McLuhan's concept of a "global village" did not anticipate an analog/digital exchange, however. While the digital revolution has proven McLuhan's prescience, it was probably Gene Youngblood's explicit linking of what he called the *videosphere* (in his 1970 publication *Expanded Cinema*) with Pierre Teilhard de Chardin's concept of *noosphere* that best envisioned the digital revolution's connection with experimental motion pictures. Teilhard (1881–1953) was born in France and ordained a Jesuit priest in 1911. His unorthodox theological positions were at odds with Catholic doctrine and led to a strained relationship with Jesuit leaders, who forbade him from publishing his writings. Teilhard's *The Phenomenon of Man* became a best seller when it was posthumously published in 1955.

Teilhard was trained as a paleontologist who reformed Darwinian concepts of "evolution." Whereas Darwin focused on early life forms that evolved into *Homo sapiens*, Teilhard's view covered a period when Earth was but a lifeless ball of rock (somewhat like our moon), which he called the *geosphere*. This "sphere" eventually evolved into a greater, organic sphere (the one that Darwin expounded upon) called the *biosphere*, which culminated in the rise of *Homo sapiens'* communication, which eventually developed (over a half century after Teilhard's death) into what Teilhard called the *noosphere*. Today, we can see this as McLuhan's "global village" or Gene Youngblood's concept of *videosphere*.

For Teilhard, this now contemporary sphere allows human evolution to continue into what he regarded as the "Omega Point." This would be a spiritual culmination of the three spheres into a realm where all humans would become as Christ. Given his Jesuit foundations, Teilhard saw this as the final point in "human" evolution, which many readers might regard as bane rather than boon. This is a theological matter that is beyond the scope of this book, although it does bring with it a wonderful, quintessential optimism for the digital revolution, which is the subject of this concluding chapter.

To be sure, the extraordinary advent of digital technologies has changed so many areas, like automobiles, robotics, and medicine, that our focus on motion pictures is a very select, very narrow one. For example, it is rather removed from such matters as the use of cell phones and social media (such as Facebook) in the 2011 political revolutions in the Middle East and North Africa.

Le Grice

Given our methodological premises, we see the truly immense technological shifts of the digital revolution as changes not merely of degree but in kind. Allow us to begin defending this assertion by drawing upon the recent writings of the remarkable British experimental film/video artist and historian Malcolm Le Grice.

Le Grice's book *Abstract Film and Beyond* was published in 1977. Though predating the digital age, it is a superb history of experimental motion pictures, which covers not just the United States but also the United Kingdom and Europe. However, it is his second book,

Experimental Cinema in the Digital Age (a collection of a number of his articles published in 2001), that is rich in resources, such as this insight into classic broadcast television (circa 1970):

> TV has, or can call on, a mass of data stored in televisual form. The proportion of material in transmission to material in store is infinitesimal. . . . It always seems to be assumed that the only method of increasing choice for the TV user is to increase the number of channels. This is a dead-end approach. It can never go far enough. It is linked to the error of relating TV production to TV transmission which leads to competitive duplication of low-quality entertainment on every channel rather than an expansion of real variety. These preconceptions grow from the accident of TV being developed as a branch of radio (broadcasting) rather than, say, the telephone system or, for that matter, the whole field of audiovisual storage not being incorporated into the library conception at an early stage.[1]

Le Grice began teaching at St. Martin's School of Art almost directly after graduating from the Slade in 1965. In the subsequent academic posts that he has held and his various associations with British Film Institute and Arts Council committees, he has continually helped to provide a practical context for experimental cinema in the United Kingdom. Le Grice helped to set up the developing and printing facilities at the London Film-makers' Co-op in the late 1960s, and during the early part of his career, his central involvement in the co-op provided a model for collective practice. At that time, a significant difference between the English filmmakers and their American counterparts was the degree to which the latter were working much more independently and in what P. Adams Sitney saw as a "visionary" tradition.[2]

Throughout Le Grice's publications, he iterates a foil to experimental motion pictures, namely what André Bazin had called the "royal road of cinema," the major genre of the fictive narrative. While we see two other major genres as coordinate to the fictive feature, Le Grice sees a binary battle between the category of this truly royal road (perhaps partnered by nonfiction works) and his own métier: experimental/avant-garde productions. Narrative in general may rather be "hardwired" in human mentation. Most ancient works, such as the

Iliad and the *Odyssey* and the biblical book of Genesis, are narratives. (Of course, there are countless "ancient works," like the *Tao Te Ching* or the *I Ching*, that are not narrative.) But consider that perhaps all of the history of drama—which is much older than the history of motion pictures—is narrative. As Christian Metz writes in *Film Language*, "In the realm of the cinema, all non-narrative genres—the documentary, the technical film, etc.—have become marginal provinces, border regions so to speak, while the *feature-length film of novelistic fiction*, which is simply called a 'film,'—the usage is significant—has traced more and more clearly the king's highway of filmic expression."[3]

More, in this same cinesemiotic book, Metz's second chapter is one of the earliest examples of what is today called *narratology*. Titled "Notes toward a Phenomenology of the Narrative," it ends with a terse definition of the very term/concept *narrative* as "a closed discourse that proceeds by unrealizing a temporal sequence of events." To be sure, while Metz's chapter concludes with this brief description, each of his terms in the definition is clearly defined in the previous pages of the chapter. For example, the term *discourse* is remarkably technical: "Every narrative is, therefore, a discourse (the converse is not true; many discourses are not narratives—the lyric poem, the educational film, etc.)." But even more insightful is the following distinction: "A beginning and an ending—that is to say, the narrative is a *temporal sequence*, one must hasten to specify: there is the time of the thing told and the time of the telling."[4]

Perhaps it is this that frustrates Le Grice? Maybe, but more likely it is the very formulaic motion picture (as opposed to novel or stage) construction of narrative, the perhaps innate but more likely arbitrary employ of what has been, since before Charlie Chaplin, typically termed *classical continuity*. In motion pictures, the "time of the telling" is tightly established. When Metz wrote *Language and Cinema* (before video or digital existed), one could simply look at a 400-foot 16mm reel mounted on a projector (likely set at twenty-four frames/second) and confirm that it would run twelve minutes. The "time of the thing told," on the other hand, would likely be greater, or it could be the same (we believe that *High Noon* was so constructed), or it could be less (*An Occurrence at Owl Creek Bridge* comes to mind) due to the fact that every cut, every edited joining of two "shots," will manifest either a continuity or a discontinuity of diegetic space and/ or time. Thus, from Metz we learn that much of the joy of narrative motion pictures derives from this fictive differential.

To be sure, we would agree that most experimental motion pictures discussed in this edition of *Direct Theory* strive to discover and explore alternative ways of constructing a "film" in a manner that does not depend upon a (well-defined) concept of narrative, including its seemingly arbitrary (but almost ubiquitous) patterns of classical continuity. But, then, Le Grice has written that he does not regard himself as a theorist. Yet, what he does as an artist/historian is provide us with a very heuristic contribution, which is glimpsed in this quotation from his 2001 book, *Experimental Cinema in the Digital Age*: "Theory for the practicing artist is not strictly scientific in method. Its place in relationship to practice is, if prioritised, secondary rather than primary. The practical work is not simply equivalent to the experiment which proves or disproves the theory. While it might seek 'generality' . . . its most consistently valuable function has been in stimulating, generating and critically guiding the development of practice."[5]

Also in the same book, in an essay titled "The Implication of Digital Systems for Experimental Film Theory," Le Grice presents a key issue for any experimental productions based not on early analog but on now-standard digital devices. We appreciate (and share) Le Grice's investigation of medium specificity. More, Le Grice explicitly refers to (Saussurian) semiotics:

> It is in the relationship to the last of [the theoretical positions that I have come to hold] that the attitude towards technology needs to be clarified. Consistent with the fundamental "tenet" of twentieth-century art, evident in the plastic arts and music but rarely in mainstream film, is the concept that there can be no convenient separation between the material "means" of a work and its meaning—that meanings derive from the working of the material. This is a concept similar to that of semiologists, that there can be no separation between the production of a thought and the operations in language.[6]

Le Grice's three theoretical positions are, briefly, "to promote the spectator as an 'active' rather than 'passive' participant"; to "problema[tize] illusion, metaphor, and narrative"; and "to stress the material conditions of production and viewing of works both as a basis of practice and a strategy of narrative identification."[7] Le Grice also writes about interactivity:

> Though the computer need not always involve interactivity in the execution of a program, it is fundamentally structured to respond to input as well as output. As with arbitrary (or random) access structures in memory, the implications for artistic practice of incorporating performance feedback by the artist or, more radically, the action of the spectator in the sequential development of a work creates significant new possibilities for art practice. It also creates significant new issues for the understanding of the relationship between the work and the spectator and for the concept of authorship which may also be seen as intrinsic to digital media.[8]

Recall how, in chapter 5, works such as J. J. Murphy's *Print Generation* were virtually predicated upon such cinematically specific characteristics as A and B winds and analog duplication's intrinsic depletion of information recorded on the film's cellulose acetate frames. Likewise, chapter 6's address of experimental video exhibits such works as Peter Campus's *Three Transitions*, which depends upon such video-specific technologies as an offscreen real-time monitor. Of course, digital technology—unlike film technology—can also allow a subject instant observation of what is being recorded. But our technostructural expectations for digital devices that we place in our major genre of experimental motion pictures must be employed in ways that transcend both analog film and analog video.

Le Grice outlines three "cinematographic technologies"; the first he calls "Photochemical/Mechanical" and the second "Analog Electronic." One can only applaud him for the prescience of his third category, "Digital Electronic." His definition is terse: "The application of computer and microprocessor technologies where images are recorded as discrete items of data (or data subject to defined algorithms) and their sequence is a matter of specific address within the context of Random Access Memory."[9] These are all very sophisticated characteristics. For example, arbitrary access, he says, "has little to do with randomization or chance."[10] Instead, he explains this one intrinsic characteristic of the new digital media as follows:

All address locations are conceptually equidistant. The computer does not [have to] walk past house numbers 2, 3, 4 and 5 to get from 1 to 6—number 1 is as close to number 1000 as it is to [number] 2. . . . This form of storage is known as Random Access Memory [RAM]. The use of the term "random" here is confusing as it has little to do with randomization or chance. The term "arbitrary" in its classical sense of "chosen" expresses this concept better. Whatever terms are used to describe this, if seen as an intrinsic property of digital media, it has radical implications for art, structures of aesthetic expression and representation. The principles on which data, information, or fragments of the represented world may be combined are only limited by the systems which can be defined for creating links, and these systems are clearly not confined to simple linearity.[11]

Again, we have not sought to address the entire scope of digital innovations for moving images, such as the Internet, cell phones, games, and so on. Rather, we are building upon *Direct Theory*'s technical/structural characteristics, such as the autonomy of the artist's acollaborative construction, economic independence, brevity, use of the phenomenology of mental imagery, an avoidance of verbal language, and an exploration of nonnarrative structures. We would like to add to these characteristics a penchant for abstraction. Following the great tradition of abstraction that began in the European avant-garde and continued through the wonderful work of Oskar Fischinger into the cinevideo productions of the West Coast Optical School in the 1960s, digital computers provide the contemporary artist with yet another tool. With the exception of cameraless animation—drawing, painting, or scratching directly onto exposed clear or black leader—motion pictures have been predicated upon Newtonian concepts of the lens. Further, even the early cameraless experiments of animators such as Len Lye and Norman McLaren (and of Man Ray, who scattered opaque and translucent objects on unexposed 35mm film stock and then flashed it and developed it) were predicated upon the intermittent (single) frame and, again, the projector lens. But computer displays on a monitor can be intrinsically lensless, and that opens up a whole new digital image-making world. Thus, the examples we now present are truly cameraless and lensless. The artist provides a computer with an algorithmic command, which the computer can display as either sound or image. What follows is but a small sample of moving images that are predicated on innovations in technologies, which are digitally specific yet still seem to be part of the major genre that we earlier termed experimental film/video.[12] We have chosen to present most of the comments on the works in the artists' own words. Our first example, *Siembra:VideoCodeo3*, is the work of two Argentinean artists.

Ivanoff and Jiménez

Below is the (somewhat edited) artists' biography they submitted:

Iván Ivanoff is an artist and self-taught programmer and researcher. As producer in new technologies and new media, his way of thinking about the world, technology and art transcends current trends, always searching for a new way to communicate and relate within the society of the future. He worked as research and development manager in different media labs based in Buenos Aires, New York and Italy, where he became acquainted with José Jiménez, a self-taught independent designer from the city of Neuquén.

Together they set up the artistic group known as **i2off.org+ r3nder.net** to carry out multimedia works focused on the poetry of the contents through their intimate experience with digital technology. The final work is expressed in different parts: text, installation, graphic piece, web piece, video, or software.

With their artistic group they appear in various parts of the world and they keep researching and developing their own technology, both software and hardware. Some years after they met they created "Estado Lateral Media Lab" (www.estadolateral.net), together with Enrique Mármora. They specialize in innovation, exploration and expansion in vanguard communications, creating multimedia experiences that are unique in their country.

In 2008 Jiménez started, with Andrea Jiménez, a festival of art, new trends and technologies: "Tratado de Integración" (www.tratadodeintegracion.cc). TDI is a festival, forum and presentation that takes place once a year in the city of Neuquén, with the purpose of showing a general view of contemporaneous new visual presentations.

Siembra:VideoCodeo3, made in 2007 by Ivanoff and Jiménez, is an experimental digital motion picture built around a unique, almost organic abstraction, which is interspersed with some Euclidian geometric shapes. Both sound and image result from a homogenization of a set of algorithms that uses a generative process. The following is a statement by the artists:

> This video is a follow up to our previous work titled *Ramas*. It was entirely generated by code (programmed structures) and it attempts to become both a visual and sound metaphor for the text that accompanies the piece. The resulting artwork is a system, a set of algorithms that process and generate the video frame by frame, based on the interaction of the various programmed agents. These behave in an autonomous and independent way, but comprise a large organism at the global ecosystem level. This work, which was completely created in Processing [a computer language], uses as generative elements three other words besides the title of the piece. These words operate as seeds, that once planted, determine, together with the virtual environment generated by the algorithms, the growth of the different elements, their state and evolution, camera positioning [Ivanoff has explained that they use "camera" as a concept; there is no physical camera], frame composition and sound.[13]

Because much of the aesthetic of *Siembra:VideoCodeo3* escapes verbal description, we call the readers' attention to plate 7.1.[14]

Because plate 7.1 is a composite of stills, the reader will not be able to experience the remarkable blend of sound and graphic transformations—it is quite ineffable. For one thing, the work is punctuated by an extraordinary sense of organic movement and the exploration of depth (*z*-axis). The digital work is bi-collaborative, brief (four minutes and nine seconds), and quintessentially nonnarrative.

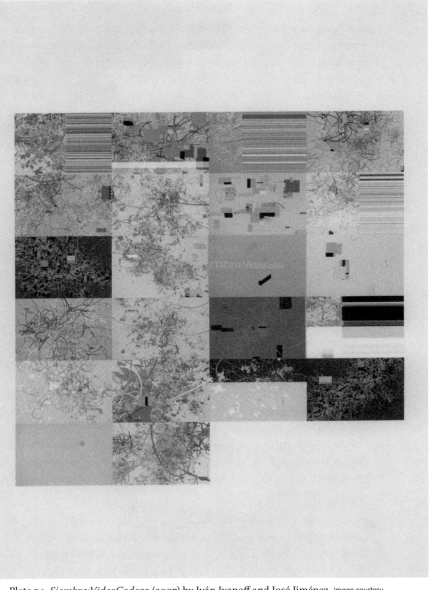

Plate 7.1. *Siembra:VideoCode03* (2007) by Iván Ivanoff and José Jiménez. Image courtesy of Estado Lateral.

Simon Payne

Simon Payne is a British artist who maintains an accessible website that contains production notes and bibliographic data and also allows the reader quick access to his extant works. Let us begin with the first work we were able to examine: *Iris Out* (2008).

As plate 7.2 illustrates, Payne's patterns in *Iris Out* are more Euclidian than those of Ivanoff and Jiménez's *Siembra:VideoCode03*. We are struck by the extraordinary rapid flicker frequency that recalls the Whitney brothers' films, specifically John Whitney Sr.'s early adoption of analog computer technologies. *Iris Out* also seems like a digital color version of flicker films such as *Alpha Mandala*. However, *Alpha Mandala* depended upon a twenty-four-frames-per-second projection of a simple white disc, interspersed with black frames. The fundamental difference of *Iris Out* is that there are no black frames, which allows for a much faster flicker frequency than cellulose acetate motion picture stock and projection. Thus, *Iris Out* is digitally specific.

On his website, Payne supplies the following biography[15]: "Simon Payne studied Time-Based Media at the Kent Institute of Art and Design in Maidstone, and Electronic Imaging at Duncan of Jordanstone College of Art. He recently completed a PhD at the Royal College of Art in London, which investigates aspects of digital aesthetics in the context of experimental film and video. His work has been screened in numerous festivals, exhibitions and venues." Regarding generic categorization, Payne's work is acollaborative, is brief (ten minutes), avoids verbal language, and has absolutely no hint of narrative, being rather a rapid flashing of colored Euclidian forms.

Below are several insightful excerpts from a message written by Payne in response to Richard Housh's request for some of his thoughts on digital-specificity:

> It's a digital palette that I'm dealing with. The colours that I've used in these works are the three primary and secondary colours, plus white and black, that constitute the SMPTE [Society of Motion Picture & Television Engineers] colour bars test signal image (i.e., white, yellow, cyan, green, magenta, blue, red and black). So in that respect they are "video specific" as much

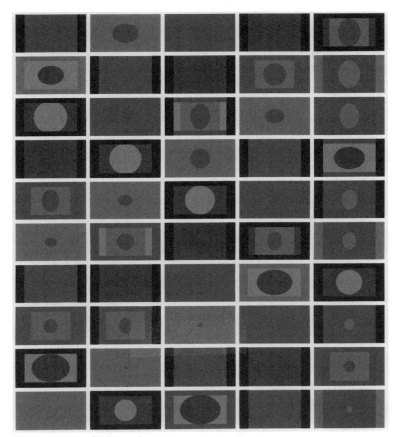

Plate 7.2. *Iris Out* by Simon Payne. Copyright © 2008 Simon Payne.

as digital specific. They couldn't, though, have been made in the days of analogue video, for various technical reasons, including the intensity of the editing, and in any case the colour palette in a digital environment is obviously very specific (i.e., yellow, cyan, green . . . etc. all have a unique numerical value in the context of the digital RGB colour space that one uses) which is significant because on some level the viewer can see/tell/understand the fact that the work is built on a limited colour palette (with hues that are of discrete values) at the same time that they can't at all account for the innumerable colours that they might see (mixed on screen? in the eye/brain?) when they're watching the work. And this seems like an interesting effect . . . because it's unsettling to some degree, and hopefully, on some level, prompts the viewer to considerations regarding perception (i.e. their relation to "the object" of perception, hence their own participation in the experience of the work, etc.). I suppose I'm interested in making work that is reflexive in that sense. Thinking about digital specificity, I guess these particular pieces also involve a tension between the capacity of human vision and the nominal precision of digital imaging. And that goes for motion perception as much as colour perception.

Thinking about motion perception there are certainly filmmakers who have explored similar aesthetics, like Walther Ruttmann's *Opus III* or Fischinger's *Radio Dynamics* or Tony and Beverly Conrad's *Straight and Narrow* (for shifting abstract stripe patterns) or Paul Sharits and Peter Kubelka (for "flicker"), and I have to say my thinking is filmic—i.e., frame-based—in many respects, in that structures are worked out based on sequences involving numbers of frames—and the basic unit that I've used most is the frame, rather than the pixel. In which case, maybe it goes back to the palette (i.e., perhaps it's the use of computer-generated digital colour within a frame-based structure) that makes it specifically digital.

Another concern specific to digital media regards projection/screen technologies, which vary in numerous ways—a CRT produces an image very differently to LCD, DLP, etc., which are all in turn very different to 16 or 35mm projection. I can't say much more on that point, apart from to say that it's something that one has to be aware of. . . . I'm not really seeking to make works that uncover or demonstrate any of the processes and characteristics associated with digital technology—and I haven't any real interest in programming or generative software, which might be where digital media is most unique—but the aesthetics of the videos that I've discussed here do result from working with a certain technology, in a way that seems fitting.[16]

W. S. Cheng

Our final example of a digital experimental motion picture artist can perhaps be best categorized by our own coinage: *neo-minimalism*. The title is *Study No. 14* (2010), and the artist is W. S. Cheng, who was born in Taipei, Taiwan, in 1979 but came to reside in the United States. He was educated at the University of Kansas, at the California Institute of the Arts (CalArts), where he earned his MFA in animation, and then at Sint-Lukas Brussels University College of Art and Design in what is now called the Transmedia program. He also worked at Montreal's National Film Board of Canada (the home of one of the world's greatest and most innovative animators: Norman McLaren).[17]

Cheng writes that he is "a visual artist working in the tradition of Absolute Animation." Further, he considers himself "particularly drawn to the concept of time, and finding new ways to arrange, compose, and develop audio/visual (e.g., temporal) structure":

> Archive, exhibition, and research are the aims of my work. My animations are collected by academic institutions, research centers, galleries, and museums. I describe *Study No. 14* as a technical exercise on pattern and timing. The work first stemmed from the parameters in music/sound (e.g., pitch, tone, dynamics, and timbre) and the concept of Expanded Cinema/Media. The computer was/is my tool of choice to create and disseminate/present "data." Hence, I see *Study No. 14* as a piece of "data" that can be used for archive, exhibition, and research. *Study No. 14* was screened twice at Anthology Film Archives under the program "New Experimental Animation." . . . Like all of my work, *Study No. 14* aims to extend the history and tradition of Absolute Animation.

To be sure, we note that Cheng's *Study No. 14* is brief (six and a half minutes) and basically acollaborative. Only two other people worked on it: a University of Kansas student, Josh Fry, reduced the initial cut by about 10 percent, getting (says Cheng) "rid of the fat," and a teacher/artist in the Department of Film and Media Studies, Robert Hurst, developed the work's curious soundtrack, in which some of the sounds are at a frequency that escapes most viewer's audition, even when they can see speakers pulsing. Otherwise, *Study No. 14* was fully funded from Cheng's own pocket and eschews verbal language except for credits at the beginning and ending. The work has been released on DVD, and its cover bears the emblem of three "frames," which could operate as the type of *pictos* that mark Michael Snow's classic minimalist film, which is sometimes referred to, in verbal language, as *Back & Forth* but perhaps more often as a single, simple grapheme of a double-headed arrow: ⟵⟶.

Study No. 14 is even more of an exploration of nonnarrative structures than is Snow's film, which is quite representational and even contains at least the fleeting suggestion of live characters, which would be essential to any hint of narrative. (Basically *Back & Forth* was filmed in a Fairleigh Dickinson University classroom in a single take during which the tripod-mounted camera—which was in the very back of the classroom—pans horizontally [back and forth] and finally tilts [up and down].)

In contrast, Cheng's work is quintessentially abstract. Only viewers who retain a penchant for anthropomorphizing (say) a painting by Jackson Pollock, or perhaps seeing the intrinsic metamorphosis of common clouds as animals, or seeing random wood grain patterns as human faces could "project" some kind of potentially narrative "characters" in *Study No. 14*'s simple—but never simplistic—core abstraction of three boxes, each containing four horizontal white lines upon a pure black background. By virtue of these key characteristics of our concept of direct theory, *Study No. 14* clearly falls within our major genre of experimental motion pictures. Even though its minimalist forms might be approximated with celluloid film or videotape, the actual work is digitally specific by virtue of the fact that the result of the use of any such analogous medium would look quite different. The work is also quite ineffable in its quiet permutations, which are excerpted in plate 7.3.

While it is difficult to generalize from but three (selected) works, we urge the reader to visit the specific websites that display these works—and others by the same artists—with their actual movements, sounds, and colors. And while our simple "triad" does reveal characteristics, such as a penchant for abstraction, for our technostructural historiography of experimental motion pictures' entrance into the digital age, we must point out that we are indeed only at the entrance, on the cusp. In 1965, Gordon Moore (who became cofounder of Intel) made

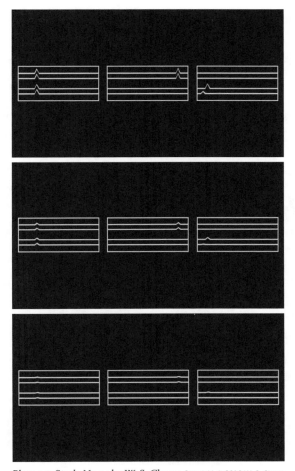

Plate 7.3. *Study No. 14* by W. S. Cheng. Copyright © 2010 W. S. Cheng

a prediction that is known as "Moore's Law." That year was before the "digital revolution," but Moore's Law (which Moore himself expects to last at least another two decades) contends that "data density" in computer technology will double every eighteen months. As we write this, the technology of the digital revolution grows smaller, cheaper, and faster at a breathtaking velocity. With that in mind, we present our research as but a "heads-up" for the future and as a confirmation of Raymond Fielding's technostructural historiography.

NOTES

SELECT BIBLIOGRAPHY

INDEX

Notes

Introduction

1. Qtd. in Allen and Gomery, *Film History*, 112.
2. Fielding, introduction, n.p.
3. Saussure, *Course in General Linguistics*, 16.
4. Ibid., 112–13.
5. Ibid., 116–17.
6. Raman Selden and Peter Widdowson, *A Reader's Guide to Contemporary Literary Theory*, 3rd ed. (Lexington: University of Kentucky Press, 1993), 104.

1. Experimental Motion Pictures as Direct Theory

1. Andrew, *Major Film Theories*, 5.
2. Bazin, *What Is Cinema?*, 15.
3. Saussure, *Course in General Linguistics*, 16.
4. Metz, *Film Language*, 123.
5. Andrew, *Major Film Theories*, 6.
6. Eisenstein, *Film Form*, 60; his emphasis.
7. Arnheim, *Visual Thinking*, 13.
8. Ibid., 148.
9. Michael S. Gazzaniga, "The Split Brain in Man," *Scientific American* 217.2 (August 1967): 29.
10. Saussure, *Course in General Linguistics*, 68.
11. Ibid.
12. Ibid., 112.
13. Barthes, *Semiotic Challenge*, 4; his emphasis.
14. Ibid., 157; our emphasis.
15. Le Grice, *Abstract Film and Beyond*, 153.
16. Christian Metz, personal letter, Paris, July 1, 1985.
17. Carl Jung, *The Structure and Dynamics of the Psyche*, vol. 8 of *Collected Works of C. G. Jung* (Princeton: Princeton University Press, 1960), 417–519.
18. MacDonald, *Critical Cinema*, 2–3; his emphasis.

2. Experimental Motion Pictures as Major Genre

1. MacDonald, *Critical Cinema*, 1; our emphasis.

2. This argument is more thoroughly detailed in Small's article "Literary and Film Genres: Toward a Taxonomy of Film," *Literature/Film Quarterly* 8.4 (1979): 290–99.

3. Animation, however, is transgeneric. Strictly speaking, animation is a technique (of single-frame cinematography), not a genre. The animated cartoon is a likely candidate for a major genre, but animation is a technique employed by all genres. Consider the animated maps in documentaries, the animated models in *2001*, and the diverse modes of animation employed by television commercials and music videos. Further, experimental production's embrace of technical innovations is highly interrelated with animation. See Russett and Starr's *Experimental Animation*.

4. Renan, *Introduction to the American Underground Film*, 17; his emphasis. We are indebted to this out-of-print study not only for a number of our provisional characteristics but also because it provided a genuine foundation for academic interest in this special body of films.

5. This first and the following seven generic characteristics have been published in slightly different fashion as part of Small's chapter "Film and Video Art" in editor Gary Edgerton's *Film and the Arts in Symbiosis* (New York: Greenwood Press, an imprint of Greenwood Publishing Group, Inc., Westport, CT, 1988).

6. Curtis's *Experimental Cinema* unfortunately also remains out of print.

7. Renan, *Introduction to the American Underground Film*, 25.

8. Ibid., 36.

9. For a far more detailed discussion of this important point, see Small's essay "Avant-Garde Silent Films" in editor Frank N. Magills's *Silent Films* (Englewood Cliffs, N.J.: Salem Press, 1982).

10. Renan, *Introduction to the American Underground Film*, 34.

11. Metz calls these "the time of the telling" and "the time of the thing told," respectively; see *Film Language*, 18.

12. Alan Williams's "Is a Radical Genre Criticism Possible?" also argued for the same trichotomy, which he called "principal film genres," independent of and five years after Small's *Literature/Film Quarterly* essay; see the *Quarterly Review of Film Studies* 9.2 (Spring 1984).

3. The European Avant-Garde

1. Eisenstein, *Film Form*, 125. This retrospective and rather conciliatory essay, "Film Form: New Problems," was written in 1935, after the advent of Soviet Socialist realism, which discredited Eisenstein's many experiments with intellectual montage.

2. Metz, *Film Language*, 18. Metz's translated *signifier* and *significate* are derived from Saussure's key semiotic terms/concepts *signifiant* (e.g., the letters/phonemes the reader now regards) and *signifié* (e.g., the actual mentation from the same regard). For both Saussure and Metz, the resulting amalgam of *sign* inextricably bonds signifier and significate (more typically translated as *signified*).

3. Perhaps the best study of these pronounced similarities between Léger's many cubist (and futurist) paintings and select frames from *Ballet Mécanique* is Lawder's *Cubist Cinema*. Lawder also cataloged (photographically) every shot in the film, perhaps using a MOMA print, seeking to provide a precise synopsis. Like many early films, there are a number of versions of the *Ballet Mécanique* floating around, each one claiming more or less to be "authentic," with scenes in different order or even missing entirely. However, in 1975, a print of the film was discovered that has a legitimate right to be considered definitive. In November of that year, Frederick Kiesler's widow, Lillian, found an ancient can of hand-spliced film in the closet of their weekend home in Germany. On the can was a label: "Leger." The cans found their way to Jonas Mekas, a filmmaker, scholar, and director of Anthology Film Archives in New York, who realized that this was Léger's personal print of the film, the one that Kiesler most likely had presented at the world premiere. The image quality was, in Mekas's words, "fantastic." See http://www.soundonsound.com/sos/sep02/articles/balletmecanique.asp.

4. For further discussion of this reflexive relationship between montage and animation in *Ballet Mécanique*, see Edward S. Small and Eugene Levinson, "Toward a Theory of Animation," *Velvet Light Trap* 24 (Fall 1989): 67–74.

5. Lawder, *Cubist Cinema*, 49.

6. While the term *rayogram* is more common to current literature, Chuck Berg's "Man Ray Creates the Rayograph" convinces us that *rayograph* is historically more accurate. Berg's essay details the development of this reflexive form. See Frank N. Magill, ed., *Great Events from History II: Arts and Culture* (Pasadena: Salem Press, 1993), 513–17.

7. Bazin, *What Is Cinema?*, 9–16. It should be noted that the particular essay "The Ontology of the Photographic Image" was written in 1945 and is partially a reaction to the direct theory of earlier EAG productions.

8. Kracauer, *Theory of Film*, 79.

9. Sitney, *Visionary Film*, 4. Sitney follows this paragraph with a superb synopsis of the film.

10. Renan, *Introduction to the American Underground Film*, 66.

11. Curtis, *Experimental Cinema*, 32.

12. Barnouw, *Documentary*, 73–81.

13. Tart, *Altered States of Consciousness*, 408.

14. Eisenstein, *Film Form*, 22.

15. Sergei Eisenstein, *Film Sense*, trans. Jay Leyda (New York: Harcourt Brace Jovanovich, 1949), 87.

16. Eisenstein, *Film Form*, 72–73.

17. Personal conversation, University of Iowa, spring 1972.

18. P. Adams Sitney's introduction to his edited study *The Avant-Garde Film* (New York: New York University Press, 1978) details this directly theoretical rejection.

4. The American Avant-Garde and the American Underground

1. Curtis, *Experimental Cinema*, 39.

2. Kracauer, *Theory of Film*, 181.

3. Arnheim, *Film as Art*, 8.

4. Ibid., 21, 57.

5. Ibid., 5.

6. Curtis, *Experimental Cinema*, 41.

7. Arnheim, *Film as Art*, 110.

8. Ibid., 133.

9. Sitney, *Visionary Film*, 14.

10. Ibid. This process of self-realization brings to mind the later use of the term *psychodrama* by psychotherapists who, independent of film, had patients act out their problems as part of their therapy (e.g., the work of Fritz Perls).

11. Ibid., 11.

12. John G. Hanhardt, "The Medium Viewed: The American Avant-Garde Film," in *A History of the American Avant-Garde Cinema*, by the American Federation of Arts (New York: AFA, 1976), 44, 46.

13. The quotes by McLaren are from a number of unpublished National Film Board interoffice memos obtained by Small.

14. Renan, *Introduction to the American Underground Film*, 17.

15. Ibid., 22.

16. Arnheim, *Film as Art*, 7.

17. Andrew, *Major Film Theories*, 27.

18. Also translated as "Art does not reproduce the visible; rather, it makes visible." Originally published in Paul Klee, *Schöpferische Konfession*, edited by Kasimir Edschmid (Berlin: Erich Reiss, 1920). An English translation by Norbert Guterman is in *The Inward Vision: Watercolors, Drawings and Writings by Paul Klee* (New York: Abrams, 1959), 5.

19. Stan Brakhage, "Metaphors on Vision," special issue, *Film Culture* (Fall 1963): n.p.

20. Kracauer, *Theory of Film*, x.

21. For a more detailed discussion of such imagery, see Small's "Introduction: Cinevideo and Mental Images," *Journal of the University Film Association* 32.1–2 (Winter–Spring 1980): 3–9.

22. For a more detailed discussion of film/video theory and cognitivism, see Small's "Supplement: Cognitive Science and Cinema," *Journal of Dramatic Theory and Criticism* 6.2 (Spring 1992): 163–231.

23. Wees, *Light Moving in Time*, 78.

24. Bazin, *What Is Cinema?*, 25.

25. Eisenstein, *Film Form*, 62.

26. Bazin, *What Is Cinema?*, 45.

27. Music video exhibits multiple influences: documentaries like *Woodstock*, Hollywood musicals, other experimental productions like *Scorpio*

Rising and Fischinger's work, Scopitone jukeboxes, and 1960s lightshows. Thus, Conner's "prototypes" are, of course, but a small part of a larger whole.

28. Eisenstein, *Film Form*, 50.

29. The research of Jim Lane assures us that the subcategory of the autobiographical/diary film flourishes far beyond the genre of the American underground. For an introduction to this kind of production, which emphasizes Mekas's major contribution, see Small's "Diary-Folk Film," *Film Library Quarterly* 9.2 (1976): 35–39.

30. Renan, *Introduction to the American Underground Film*, 101; his emphasis. A similar point was made by Lewis Jacobs some two decades earlier in his 1947 essay "Experimental Cinema in America: 1921–1947," which was first published in *Hollywood Quarterly* 3.2 (Winter 1947–48). The essay also constitutes a supplement to Jacobs's *The Rise of the American Film: A Critical History* (New York: Teachers College Press, 1968); the following quote is from page 543: "Living a kind of private life of its own [experimental cinema's] concern has been solely with motion pictures as a medium of artistic expression. This emphasis upon means rather than content not only endows experimental films with a value of their own but distinguishes them from all other commercial, documentary, educational, and amateur productions."

5. Expanded Cinema and Visionary Film

1. Renan, *Introduction to the American Underground Film*, 227; his emphasis.

2. Youngblood, *Expanded Cinema*, 156.

3. Ibid., 97.

4. Allen and Gomery, *Film History*, v.

5. Youngblood, *Expanded Cinema*, 97. Such step-printer production likely served a laboratory function for MTV work such as David Orr's "Fairchild" (1988), a new-age music video comprised of step-optical, high-contrast, multilayered images of Philadelphia. Further, contemporary video technology allows greater ease and economy for such structures. Loop printing first appears in *Ballet Mécanique*; in the 1980s, it informed a number of MTV works (e.g., U2's "Desire: Hollywood Re-Mix" and the Smith's "How Soon Is Now?"). Digital looping is far cheaper and easier than O'Neill's step-printer work.

6. Youngblood, *Expanded Cinema*, 218–19.

7. Roland Barthes, *The Grain of the Voice* (New York: Hill and Wang, 1985), 20.

8. Youngblood, *Expanded Cinema*, 223. *Yantra* is hand-drawn.

9. Ibid., 41.

10. Jung, *Mandala Symbolism*, 3.

11. Ibid., 4; his emphasis.

12. Qtd. in Youngblood, *Expanded Cinema*, 159. Brakhage has said much the same about his own work.

13. Ibid., 151. One could also argue that if these forms are indeed archetypes, such putative cause and effect is really impertinent. Perhaps network

logos are mandalic for the same reason some Busby Berkeley choreographics were mandalic—which is to say for the same archetypal reason that Native American sand paintings are.

14. Arnheim, *Film as Art*, 114.

15. Bazin, *What Is Cinema?*, 14.

16. Youngblood, *Expanded Cinema*, 122.

17. Sitney, *Visionary Film*, 207.

18. Brakhage, who did not make structural films, regarded it as experimental's "longest lived" genre; Sitney's effect on its popularity seems clearly causal.

19. Sitney, *Visionary Film*, 408.

20. Ibid., 407.

21. Bazin, *What Is Cinema?*, 39.

22. Ibid., 35–36.

23. Sitney, *Visionary Film*, 412.

24. Saussure, *Course in General Linguistics*, 16.

25. Small has also elaborated the laboratory function of *Wavelength* for his article "Minimalist/Structuralist Aesthetics in MacNeil/Lehrer 'Postcards,'" *Critical Studies in Mass Communication* 3.4 (December 1986): 487–92.

26. Sitney, *Visionary Film*, 310.

27. Exceptions to fixed-camera animation can be found, such as Marie Menken's *Lights* (1965), a handheld, single-frame study of conversely quite static urban incandescent lights.

28. Eisenstein, *Film Form*, 55.

29. Ibid., 56.

30. Compare Edward S. Small and Eugene Levinson, "Toward a Theory of Animation," *Velvet Light Trap* 24 (Fall 1989): 67–74, for elaboration.

31. See Russett and Starr's *Experimental Animation*, which quotes Conrad on the work's production: "This implies some single-frame technique . . . [but] most of the work . . . [was] done through editing procedures" (153).

32. See Small and Anderson, "What's in a Flicker Film?"

33. See page 33 of the above article for six plates correlating extant mandala patterns with drawings done by an audience of artists who were asked to provide color sketches of their phenomenology while watching the film.

34. MacDonald's research was presented at the joint University Film Video Association/Society for Cinema Studies Conference (July 1988, Montana State University); his elaboration of single-take constructions in avantgarde cinema came to us in the audience as an outstanding oversight on the part of Sitney himself.

35. Compare Derrida's *Of Grammatology*, which came into English translation for the Johns Hopkins University Press the same year Murphy's *Print Generation* was completed: 1974.

36. Sitney, *Visionary Film*, 412.

37. Indeed, this historical survey is so select that it again bypasses countless films and experimental artists.

38. Herbert Zettl, *Sight, Sound, Motion: Applied Media Aesthetics* (Boston: Wadsworth Cenage Learning, 2010), 279–90; Metz, *Film Language*, 18. For example, no novel, painting, or play can ever have a jump cut. Motion picture works do have jump cuts, which can (in turn) be described in Zettl's "tertiary" movement by editing, as well as by two of Metz's "syntagmas" (namely *shot* and *scene*).

6. Experimental Video

1. Fielding, introduction, n.p.
2. Le Grice, *Abstract Film and Beyond*, 74.
3. Ibid., 32.
4. Ibid., 152.
5. Price, *Video-Visions*, 93.
6. Marshall McLuhan, *Understanding Media*, 312–13; his emphasis.
7. We would suggest that the interested reader also consult the following websites to gain some sense of the scope of international experimental video: Electronic Arts Intermix (http://www.eai.org/index.htm), Le Videographe (http://www.videographe.qc.ca/), and PRIM (http://www.primcentre.org /prim_eng.html).
8. Le Grice, *Abstract Film and Beyond*, 86.
9. Ibid., 87.
10. Ibid., 88.
11. See Price, *Video-Visions*, 213–15.
12. Stephen Beck, "Videographics: Reflections on the Art of Video," in *Video Art: An Anthology*, edited by Ira Schneider and Beryl Korot (New York: Harcourt Brace Jovanovich, 1976), 20.
13. John G. Hanhardt, "Video Art: Expanded Forms, Notes toward a History," *The Luminous Image* (Amsterdam: Stedelijk Museum, 1984), 57–58.
14. Ibid., 57.
15. Ibid., 55.
16. Ibid., 56.
17. Other permutations in *Hearts* and *Heads* are far less open to direct, reflexive understanding (although they still can covertly direct audience attention to unexplored video parameters); *Hearts* embodies electronic processing credited to an Oswego, N.Y., video lab, and *Heads* depends upon "voltage control of image parameters," according to an Electronic Arts Intermix catalog description.
18. Lori Zippay, ed., *Electronic Arts Intermix: Video* (New York: EAI, 1991), 172.
19. Fredric Jameson, *Postmodernism, or, the Cultural Logic of Late Capitalism* (Durham: Duke University Press, 1991), 96.
20. Zippay, *Electronic Arts Intermix*, 182.
21. Bill Viola, "Video as Art," *Journal of Film and Video* 36.1 (Winter 1984): 41.
22. Stam, *Reflexivity in Film and Literature*, 255.

23. Ibid., xii.

24. Ibid., xiv.

25. Metz, *Language and Cinema*, 74.

7. Digital Experimental Motion Pictures

1. Le Grice, *Experimental Cinema*, 217

2. From www.luxonline.org.uk/artists/malcolm_le_grice/essay(1).html. See also Simon Payne's website.

3. Metz, *Film Language*, 94.

4. Ibid., 18.

5. Le Grice, *Experimental Cinema*, 237–38.

6. Ibid., 235.

7. Ibid.

8. Ibid., 316.

9. Ibid., 236.

10. Ibid., 315.

11. Ibid., 315–16.

12. We are indebted to Richard Housh, Small's teaching assistant at the time, who discovered the works of Ivanoff and Jiménez and Simon Payne.

13. See www.i2off.org/videocode03/.

14. Ibid.

15. See http://www.simonrpayne.co.uk/.

16. Simon Payne, email message to Richard Housh, August 8, 2009.

17. The following material on Cheng is drawn from several personal interviews with him.

Select Bibliography

Allen, Robert C., and Douglas Gomery. *Film History: Theory and Practice*. New York: Knopf, 1985.

American Federation of Arts. *A History of the American Avant-Garde Cinema*. New York: AFA, 1976.

Andrew, J. Dudley. *The Major Film Theories*. New York: Oxford University Press, 1976.

Arnheim, Rudolf. *Film as Art*. Berkeley: University of California Press, 1966.

———. *Visual Thinking*. Berkeley: University of California Press, 1969.

Barnouw, Erik. *Documentary: A History of the Non-fiction Film*. New York: Oxford University Press, 1974.

Barthes, Roland. *The Semiotic Challenge*. Translated by Richard Howard. New York: Hill and Wang, 1988.

Bazin, André. *What Is Cinema?* Selected and translated by Hugh Gray. Berkeley: University of California Press, 1971.

Curtis, David. *Experimental Cinema*. New York: Universe, 1970.

Derrida, Jacques. *Of Grammatology*. Translated by G. C. Spivak. Baltimore: Johns Hopkins University Press, 1976.

Dwoskin, Stephen. *Film Is: The International Free Cinema*. New York: Overlook Press, 1975.

Eisenstein, Sergei. *Film Form [and] The Film Sense*. Edited and translated by Jay Leyda. New York: Meridian Books, 1967.

Fielding, Raymond. *The American Newsreel: 1911–1967*. Norman: University of Oklahoma Press, 1972.

———, ed. Introduction to *A Technological History of Motion Pictures and Television: An Anthology from the Pages of the "Journal of the Society of Motion Picture and Television Engineers."* Berkeley: University of California Press, 1967.

———. *The Technique of Special Effects Cinematography*. Waltham, Mass.: Focal Press, 1955.

Gardner, Howard. *The Mind's New Science: A History of the Cognitive Revolution*. New York: Basic, 1987.

Jung, C. G. *Mandala Symbolism*. Princeton: Bollingen, 1972.

Kracauer, Siegfried. *Theory of Film: The Redemption of Physical Reality*. New York: Oxford University Press, 1965.

Kuenzli, Rudolf E., ed. *Dada and Surrealist Film*. New York: Willis Locker and Owens, 1987.

Lawder, Standish. *The Cubist Cinema*. New York: New York University Press, 1975.

Le Grice, Malcolm. *Abstract Film and Beyond*. Cambridge: MIT Press, 1977.

——. *Experimental Cinema in the Digital Age*. London: BFI, 2001.

MacDonald, Scott. *A Critical Cinema*. Berkeley: University of California Press, 1988.

McLuhan, Malcolm. *Understanding Media: The Extensions of Man*. Cambridge, Mass.: MIT Press, 1994.

Mekas, Jonas. *Movie Journal: The Rise of a New American Cinema, 1959–1971*. New York: Collier Books, 1972.

Metz, Christian. *Film Language: A Semiotics of the Cinema*. Translated by Michael Taylor. New York: Oxford University Press, 1974.

——. *Language and Cinema*. Translated by Donna Jean Umiker-Sebeok. Paris: Mouton, 1974.

Munsterberg, Hugo. *The Photoplay: A Psychological Study*. New York: D. Appleton and Company, 1916. Also sometimes published under the title *The Film: A Psychological Study*.

Ornstein, Robert E., ed. *The Nature of Human Consciousness*. San Francisco: W. H. Freeman, 1973.

Peterson, James. *Dreams of Chaos, Visions of Order: Understanding the American Avant-garde Cinema*. Detroit: Wayne State University Press, 1994.

Price, Jonathan. *Video-Visions: A Medium Discovers Itself*. New York: NAL, 1977.

Renan, Sheldon. *An Introduction to the American Underground Film*. New York: Dutton, 1967.

Russett, Robert, and Cecile Starr. *Experimental Animation: Origins of a New Art*. New York: Da Capo Press, 1988.

Saussure, Ferdinand de. *Course in General Linguistics*. Translated by W. Baskin. New York: McGraw-Hill, 1966.

Schneider, Ira, and Beryl Korot, eds. *Video Art: An Anthology*. New York: Harcourt Brace Jovanovich, 1976.

Sitney, P. Adams. *Visionary Film: The American Avant-Garde*. New York: Oxford University Press, 2002.

Small, Edward S., and Joseph D. Anderson. "What's in a Flicker Film?" *Communication Monographs* 43.1 (March 1976): 29–34.

Stam, Robert. *Reflexivity in Film and Literature*. New York: Columbia University Press, 1992.

Tart, Charles, ed. *Altered States of Consciousness*. New York: Doubleday, 1969.

Teilhard de Chardin, Pierre. *The Phenomenon of Man*. New York: Harper, 1959.

Wees, William C. *Light Moving in Time: Studies in the Visual Aesthetics of Avant-Garde Film*. Berkeley: University of California Press, 1992.

Youngblood, Gene. *Expanded Cinema*. New York: Dutton, 1970.

Index

Page numbers in italics indicate illustrations. Titles of films, in italics, are followed by the name of the filmmaker or filmmakers in parentheses.

Index

Index

Edward S. Small is an emeritus professor of film and media studies at the University of Kansas. He is a motion picture theorist specializing in semiotics and a motion picture artist concentrating on experimental production.

Timothy W. Johnson's career includes English teaching, a PhD in cinema from the University of Southern California, and more than two decades as editor and production supervisor for computer and printer manuals. He is an editor and a digital media artist.